Paul Bernardo and

Karla Homolka

The Horrific True Story Behind Canada's Ken and Barbie Killers

(Real Crime by Real Killers Vol 7)

Ryan Becker and Nancy Veysey

ISBN-10: 1725125889

ISBN-13: 978-1725125889

Acknowledgements

This is a special thanks to the following readers who took time out of their busy lives to read my work and give me suggestions. Thank you all so much!

Summer Foovay, Jannis M. Fetter, Kim Gieck, A. Lanneau, Elizabeth A Norris, Robin, Leigh Morgan, rosebud, Miriam P, Mollie, Tadgad, Radar453, Linda Wheeler, A. K. Salmon, MCM, Bonnie J, Tonja Marshall, Susan Groth, Christina Riemenschneider, Kernene, Kathy Morgan, Melody Lema, Jennifer L. Varga, Sharyn Thornbury, James Oliver, Bari Shepard, Penguins Rule, Rhonda Voigts, Mary, Michelle McDonald, Sandy Young

Table of Contents

Dark Fantasies
Turn Reality

Quick note from the Author

The following is a true story based on facts garnered from official documents, police reports, trial transcripts, interviews, conversations, and other sources. It is a disturbing story and the author has made the decision to withhold some details; such as the more graphic descriptions of the rapes and sexual assaults on the underage victims.

The author attempts, as always, to present the truth, while showing respect to victims and families.

Some passages are creative interpretations used by the author based on known facts, and will be followed by (CI).

Thank you.

Prologue

The brutality of the crimes committed by Paul Bernardo and Karla Homolka, the rape and murder of teenage girls; one being Karla's own sister, might not cause anyone to bat an eye today. In Canada, in the latter part of the last century, however, people were stunned. First, the multiple rapes by an unknown assailant dubbed, "The Scarborough Rapist" had women terrified to be alone. Soon after, "The Schoolgirl Murders" rocked the area.

What no one expected, when authorities finally announced they had made an arrest and had a confession, was how eerily normal the felons looked. Both young, blond and tanned, the married couple were to become known as, "The Ken and Barbie Killers."

The publication ban regarding their crimes and evidence collected made them even more mysterious and intriguing.

What makes people commit such despicable acts against not just fellow humans, but their own flesh and blood? Were there other crimes Bernardo and Homolka were never charged with? Any unsolved cases of young women who were found murdered, or never found at all? Was Paul Bernardo controlling Karla and she was just another victim, or was she the puppet master?

These are a few of the questions that have plagued me since I first heard of the deadly duo and their crimes twenty-plus years ago. I will attempt to shed some light on the two from my own research and maybe find a few answers.

I do think most of the answers will go with Bernardo, Homolka, and their victims to the grave.

Join me if you dare.

ONE

\-------------------------

Tammy

*P*aul loves Tammy

Tammy loves Paul

Mrs. Paul Bernardo

Tammy Bernardo

Tammy had a crush.

She sighed deeply as she scrawled in a notebook in large, loopy handwriting favored by crushing, teenage girls. The radio in her bedroom played a love ballad as she daydreamed about her oldest sister, Karla's, boyfriend. She really liked Paul. She knew he liked her, too. He had told her.

Maybe she should have felt guilty about the stolen kisses the two had shared, but she couldn't bring herself to. She loved Karla, but she could be a real pain. Always flaunting her looks, her boyfriend, anything she thought might make her baby sister jealous, and most of the time, it worked. Not this time though.

Tammy could still see Karla's angry face and hear her ear-piercing screeches when she and Paul had shown up several hours after leaving to go on a beer run. Karla cursed at Tammy while Tammy had inwardly smiled to herself. It had felt amazing that her big sister was actually jealous of her, for once. And no wonder, Paul was a great catch.

Tall and blond, he had a great job, and a rad sports car. During their outing, in between chugging beers and making out, Paul had told Tammy how much more beautiful and desirable he found her. She did not need to bleach her naturally fair locks, and her body was much firmer and toned. Next to her, Karla was a fat old cow.

Karla still thought they would be married one day, but there was nothing to worry about, he assured Tammy. She belonged to him and he planned on having her forever. As she looked out the window of her bedroom, watching for the first glimpse of his car pulling into the driveway, she knew she would do anything for Paul. She loved Paul so much, she could just die. (CI)

The snow drifted down slowly. It was to be a white Christmas; nothing unusual for St. Catherine's, Ontario. It was the night before Christmas Eve, 1990, and festivities were in full swing in a suburban home a few miles from Niagara Falls. Upstairs in the split level house, a mother, father, and their middle daughter slept, perhaps while visions of sugar plums danced in their heads.

Earlier, everyone had gathered to partake in spiked eggnog and other mixed drinks. Unbeknownst to parents Karel and Dorothy, their eldest daughter, Karla, had added about 50mg of the prescription sedative Halcion to drinks she had prepared for her youngest sister, Tammy. Her middle sister, Lori, noticed that Tammy seemed a bit buzzed and told Karla to stop giving Tammy alcohol. Upset that she was being ignored, Lori went to bed, followed shortly after by her parents.

Tammy, beginning to feel the effects of the combination of sedatives and alcohol, went upstairs to grab a bite to eat. She hoped the food would sober her up a bit. She did not want to fall asleep and miss the movie Karla had rented. It turned out it would not be the movie rental that was the showcase of the evening. It would be the movie made starring Tammy, and all that occurred during and after which changed so many lives forever, and ended the life of one person.

Downstairs in the den, fifteen-year-old Tammy Homolka continued partying with her older sister, Karla, and Karla's boyfriend, Paul. Tammy and Karla's parents were not prudish when it came to their children drinking. Even if they were not around to personally supervise things, they felt Karla and Paul

13

could be trusted to take care of Tammy, and as long as they were drinking at home, their parents reasoned, they were safe. That night in 1990, nothing could be further from the truth.

Born in St. Catherine's, Ontario, Canada, on January 1, 1976, the youngest of three girls, Tammy was a bubbly blond, whose large doe eyes gleamed through a fringe of platinum bangs. 'Tow headed,' is what old-timers used to call children with hair like Tammy's so blond it was almost white. Tammy excelled at sports and had a trim, fit physique that any girl, even her sister, Karla, would kill to have.

Paul would flirt with Tammy, teasing her that she pretended not to know the effect she had on him. Tammy giggled as Paul wrapped her in his arms and kissed her on the cheek. Karla was not amused in the least. She loved her sister, but she loved Paul more and seethed with anger that her little sister had something Paul wanted that Karla could never give him. Tammy was still a virgin, and Tammy's virginity was what Karla planned on giving her boyfriend for Christmas.

Karla had attempted to present her boyfriend with that gift before, but her plan had been derailed when Tammy woke suddenly from the Valium Karla had mixed in her spaghetti. Karla, who worked at a veterinary clinic, had stolen some of the sedative and drugged Tammy. After eating the spiked food, Tammy had passed out and Paul had begun undressing her, and preparing to rape her when she suddenly regained consciousness. Infuriated,

Paul stormed from the room, while a confused Tammy was coaxed by her sister to disrobe and go to bed. She must have been extremely tired, said Karla, since she practically fell asleep eating dinner.

Confused but unquestioning, Tammy took her older sister's advice. Moving as if she were in a daze and her limbs feeling heavy and limp like a ragdoll, Tammy managed to remove her clothes and crawl under her thick comforter. As she passed out once again into dreamless unconsciousness, she had no idea someone was watching her. Paul Bernardo stood over her sleeping body and masturbated. It was not as satisfying as the rape he had planned earlier, but it would have to do until he got another opportunity.

December 23, 1990, was the chance Paul had been waiting for. A few weeks earlier he had taken Tammy on a beer run, which had ended up taking several hours. He had admitted to Karla that he had used the opportunity to make out with Tammy, but did not dare to take it any farther than kissing and heavy petting. Besides, it was rape, not consensual sex that gave Paul his kicks. He wanted Tammy desperately, now more than ever after their make out session, but he craved the physical brutality and control raping someone gave him.

Paul had waited, biding his time, often resorting to standing outside Tammy's window and masturbating as she changed clothes. Tonight was going to be different, however. Tonight, he would possess Tammy physically. With Karla's help, Paul would take what he desired.

Logs popped and crackled in the downstairs den's large fireplace. Tammy was consuming a far greater amount of alcohol than either Paul or Karla. Karla kept refreshing her sister's drink and Tammy, feeling mature and happy to be included in activities with two adults who were treating her as a peer, kept drinking, not wanting the fun to end.

Soon Tammy was getting sleepy and having a difficult time keeping her eyes open. The room listed and began to spin as a wave of nausea swept over the teen. Karla, playing nursemaid, comforted her younger sister and reassured her that she would feel much better after a nap. She and Paul would not ditch her, Karla said. They would stay with Tammy the entire time.

That is exactly what the couple did. As Tammy passed out from the alcohol she had consumed, Karla got the next part of the plan ready. She had once again used her job at the veterinary clinic to obtain a drug she hoped would keep her sister unconscious until Paul could complete the act this time.

At work, Karla had seen the effects of a drug called Halothane; used as an anesthetic for surgical procedures. Halothane's sedative effects were closely monitored in the clinic, however, where supplemental oxygen would be used, as well as a flow meter to measure the amount of Halothane given. Patients given Halothane are often intubated; meaning a tube is inserted orally to keep the airway patent. Karla knew the dangers of the drug being used in a non-clinical setting and the increased sedative effects when combined with alcohol.

Paul grabbed his video camera, a different one from the one he had been using earlier to tape the entire Homolka family as they drank eggnog and kidded around. Focusing the lens on Tammy, Paul instructed Karla to help him undress Tammy. The couple took turns raping Tammy, and it would all be caught on film.

Karla held the Halothane-soaked cloth tightly to Tammy's nose and mouth, fearful of Tammy regaining consciousness; like their previous attempt. Instead of regaining consciousness, Tammy began to vomit, sending Paul and Karla into a panic. Further adding to the frantic situation, Tammy choked on her own vomit, aspirated, and stopped breathing.

In a flurry of activity, the couple quickly cleaned Tammy up and dressed her before calling for an ambulance. So great was their panic that instead of simply turning the den light on so they could see better, they dragged Tammy into Karla's room. Paul made a half-hearted attempt at CPR, but the little time they had before medical technicians arrived was devoted to hiding evidence and cleaning up the scene. The blanket Tammy had vomited on was thrown in the washing machine, and the bottles of Halothane and Halcion stashed out of sight.

Tammy's parents did not even realize anything was amiss until the emergency lights and sirens alerted them. As medics attempted resuscitative measures, Karla assured her parents Tammy was looking better and appeared to be regaining her color. Karel and Dorothy followed the ambulance to the hospital, while Karla, Lori, and Paul stayed behind to answer questions. Tammy would never regain consciousness and was later pronounced dead at the hospital.

The couple's story, that Tammy had become intoxicated and began vomiting from the alcohol, before losing consciousness, was suspicious, but accepted by both the family and medical staff. Despite having a chemical burn that covered the side of her face, Tammy's death was chalked up to being just a terrible accident. The medical examiner reasoned that the burn could have been caused by gastric juices Tammy expelled while vomiting. Karla said she thought it was a carpet burn Tammy received when she and Paul attempted to drag her body into a position in which they would be able to perform CPR once they realized she was no longer breathing.

Looking back, as with most extended criminal investigations, there were so many mix-ups and missed opportunities. Opportunities for the authorities to catch the perpetrators and prevent some of the future carnage that resulted from a pair of rapists and killers running loose on the streets. The Canadian government, law enforcement particularly, has been judged harshly for decisions that resulted in a frustratingly prolonged investigation in which inaccurate eyewitness testimony was relied on too heavily, while DNA that could have identified the guilty party remained untested for over two years.

The dozens of victims of the sex crimes Paul Bernardo committed, whether alone, or as he alleges, in conjunction with Karla Homolka, might have been spared the assaults they were to suffer. Leslie Mahaffy and Kristen French might still be alive with families of their own. If the crimes had been stopped with that committed against Tammy Lyn Homolka, how different would things have turned out for everyone involved? How much pain and loss could others have been spared?

It is difficult to fathom that Paul Bernardo, who would eventually be linked via DNA to the Scarborough sex crimes, was pulled in and questioned regarding the assaults on more than one occasion. Bernardo even joked with law enforcement that he could also see a resemblance between himself and a sketch of the rapist created from victims descriptions. It seemed to be just a part of his sick game — a game with deadly consequences.

Tammy was laid to rest on December 27, 1990, only a few days short of her sixteenth birthday. The funeral home had done its best to cover the large reddish-purple burn on her cheek, for it was to be an open casket service. Karla kept stroking her sister's hair, and she and Paul both kissed Tammy's cold lips, telling her how much they loved her. Not until more deaths occurred involving Paul Bernardo and Karla Homolka, would the trinkets the couple had placed in the casket be found.

When Tammy's body was exhumed, it was noted that Karla had placed a necklace around Tammy's neck; the same necklace she had been wearing in the video of Karla and Paul raping Tammy. On the necklace was a gold ring belonging to Bernardo. They had also placed photos of themselves, and an invitation to their wedding. When the authorities passed this news on to Karel and Dorothy, they asked that the items not be returned to the coffin before Tammy was once again returned to her resting place.

TWO

Paul Loses It

Paul had anticipated that Christmas 1990 would be the best of his entire life. He couldn't recall any happy childhood memories revolving around Christmas. Karla was the one person he had spoken openly with regarding how miserable his upbringing had been. His mother was a constant source of embarrassment for him, and he hated her for blurting out the news that he had been the product of an extramarital affair.

Karla had planned so meticulously how she would obtain her Christmas gift of Tammy for Paul. She had begun researching prescription sedatives and decided that the drug Halcion would be the safest to administer. Using her youth and her looks, she had visited male physicians, who she found sympathetic to her complaints of insomnia and was able to obtain multiple prescriptions.

When Tammy died, Paul blamed Karla for her death. Karla should have known the correct dosage of Halcion, she should not have held the Halothane-soaked rag directly to Tammy's face, especially for the length of time that she did. In effect, Paul fell apart psychologically and was well on his way to either a nervous breakdown or suicide.

Not only was he staring at pictures of Tammy all the time and crying uncontrollably, but he was doing so in the presence of other people. He told his friends he did not want to live without Tammy. His alcohol and drug use escalated after Tammy's death, and Karla watched her boyfriend unravel with mixed emotions.

On the one hand, if he died; from an accidental overdose or by suicide, then Karla would be free to move on, something the teenager was good at. Snagging Paul Bernardo and having him propose to her had been a rush at the time, proof she was capable of getting anyone to do anything. But the fact of the matter was, she did not love him. Well, she loved him, but she did not "love him, love him."

In addition to gaining her freedom, Karla would also garner even more sympathy from people after having just lost Tammy. That sympathy represented power to Karla; when people fawned all over her and her poor-pitiful-me act, they were ripe for manipulation. Karla could play the victim to the hilt; she had been doing it her whole life to perfect the part.

Karla was excellent at stepping back and seeing all the options laid out in front of her and anticipating other people's next move before they were even aware of what they were about to do. Paul keeping trophies, things that had belonged to Tammy, was understandable to Karla. She had read plenty of true crime books and knew that was a common trait. Keeping the clothes Tammy had worn that fateful night were one thing, but the last cereal box she had eaten from? That was taking things too far.

What if Paul anticipated the police one day figuring out the true cause of Tammy's death? Karla wondered, could he be laying the groundwork for an insanity defense? Certainly the way he would beat his head with his fists repeatedly while he wailed and cried to their friends about how much he loved and missed Tammy made him seem insane.

Paul had not only entrusted the secrets of his sad home life with Karla and the fantasies he had of abduction and rape, he had also told her about rapes he had committed before and during their relationship. Karla had tried convincing Paul that her planning and helping carry out possible future abductions and rapes would be the wise thing to do. Karla was so sure of her propensity to pull off the perfect crime, she believed her involvement would keep them out of prison.

It has been thought by some people in hindsight, that, although part of Karla's argument for being involved was telling Paul this would bring them even closer, she had no desire to salvage the dwindling relationship. Karla enjoyed calling the shots, the excitement of planning crimes, the thrill of feeling she was intellectually superior to others, that she could outsmart not only potential victims, but also law enforcement.

THREE

Karla Takes Control

Paul still was not one hundred percent on board with turning over control to Karla. He did not relish the thought of having to share every experience with someone else either. Although he would let her plan some events, such as the Kristen French abduction they would go on to commit together, sometimes Paul wanted the stalking and raping all to himself.

Paul was also an opportunist, however, and was happy to rape a woman with little time or effort expended hunting her down. Especially if she had insulted or snubbed him. More so if he was intoxicated and she turned away his advances in front of his friends.

Such was the situation one night after Paul and Karla had moved into their pink abode, where they would go on to murder Leslie Mahaffy and Kristen French. The couple had invited friends over for the usual debauchery — drinking and drugging 'til the wee hours. Paul's friend had brought along the girl he was dating and her best friend. Both girls were seventeen at the time.

Paul started out attempting to charm the girl, but as the alcohol and pills he had taken began to take effect, he became more belligerent and difficult to deal with. Only years later would Paul's friend and his girlfriend tell authorities what had occurred that night. No one had confronted Paul or Karla about what had taken place.

The seventeen-year-old, after rebuffing Paul, had made her way to a downstairs bathroom. While she was using the bathroom, Paul had pushed his way in. There, in the bathroom, he had raped the girl as she pleaded for help and begged him to stop. Paul was way too mad to stop. After the assault, the girl told the couple with whom she had gone to the Bernardo-Homolka residence what had taken place.

No one confronted Paul or called police. No one even called a cab to ferry the brutalized girl to a hospital, since everyone was too bombed to drive her anywhere themselves. Instead, they spent a sleepless night inside the same house, where she had been raped with the rapist passed out a few yards away. In the morning they all sat around the kitchen table eating fast food, no one daring to speak of the events of the previous night.

Clearly, in Karla's thinking, Paul had enjoyed himself that night and they knew they could count on those involved to keep their mouths shut, but it was yet another example of Paul's recklessness and risk-taking. She had instructed Paul to carry pantyhose in his glovebox and use them as a mask when the urge to rape struck him. Paul complied with placing them in his car, but he never used them to disguise his appearance, merely to bind the victims.

He also never used a condom; even though Karla pointed out the stupidity of his non-compliance with this particular request of hers. While he had been raping her sister, Tammy, Karla had been afraid he might impregnate the teen and that was something even she couldn't explain away. She was not worried about him impregnating the strangers he assaulted, though, instead she was concerned with the possibility he might leave DNA behind. Paul didn't share her concern. He was convinced he was careful about not leaving clues behind, and that if the police hadn't nabbed him for the crimes so far, they never would.

So certain was he in his own invincibility and the fallibility of the still relatively new science of using DNA to catch criminals that when authorities questioned him about a series of rapes, he consented willingly to their request for DNA sample. Paul Bernardo felt like one of the legendary Untouchables. Since none of the Canadian cops he encountered seemed to have the mental fortitude of the late great Elliot Ness, Bernardo had no worries.

A precaution Bernardo did occasionally take was wiping down surfaces to erase any fingerprints he might have left. It occurred to him that a better solution was not leaving fingerprints in the first place. Karla had been trying to think up gift ideas for Paul, when ironically, he came up with the idea to request the same item of clothing that would help clear O.J. Simpson of murder charges during his criminal trial: a pair of black Isotoner gloves.

Maybe Karla should have gifted herself a pair. After the abduction of Kristen French, police found a torn portion of the map used by Karla in her ruse to get Kristen away from the busy street by standing in a church parking lot where Bernardo was parked and inquiring about directions. Investigators dusted the scrap of paper for fingerprints they later identified as belonging to Karla.

For all her belief she was a criminal mastermind, Karla made one of the simplest errors possible. Now authorities knew that the year plus they had devoted to searching for the two white men in a cream colored Camaro, that witnesses said were involved in the abduction was an unforgivable mistake and a waste of precious time they would never get back.

It was a mistake among many law enforcement made that would never be forgotten.

FOUR

The Princess and the Knight-mare

"This place isn't a diner or a dive, it is a dump," she silently mused to herself, puffing her cheeks full of air that she expelled upwards towards her bleached blond bangs. The processed, frizzled hair blew up away from her forehead only slightly, since it was shellacked into place with so much hairspray that it was practically a fire hazard. Her friend sat across from her in the booth chattering away, oblivious to her friend's mood.

As she scanned the dark restaurant, several guys attempted to catch her eye. Not a chance in hell. She let loose an audible sigh of boredom. Then, as her eyes reached the entrance, she saw a man so striking, he could have been a marble statue of an ancient god come to life. "That is more like it," she purred internally.

The Adonis locked eyes with her as he pushed past the maître d' stationed at the front of the restaurant. He needed no help finding a table. He knew exactly where he was headed. Used to his buddy taking the lead, his best friend trailed along behind him silently as they approached the two women seated in the dimly-lit booth. As he got closer, she could feel the vibrations of the music that filled the air and it felt as if her entire body tingled and throbbed to the beat.

Coyly, she dropped a napkin on the floor as he approached, using the excuse to snake her long, slender leg out to try to reach the errant napkin with her foot. Catching the object with the toe of her shoe, she slowly slid her foot back under the table and bent to retrieve the napkin, displaying a great deal of cleavage, just as she had planned. Her friend giggled nervously, as she observed the events unfolding around her, having finally stopped her incessant yammering. (CI)

When Paul Bernardo and Karla Homolka met, she was seventeen and he was twenty-three. While young, Karla was far from naïve. Both had spent their lives lying to others, as well as themselves.

Karla told people one week she was going to study criminal justice and work in law enforcement. The next week, she would say she planned on studying medicine and working as a veterinarian. Paul, on the other hand, appeared to have his future laid out for him in the white collar world of investments. Both had the dreams, but not the drive.

Paul's job would soon tank and he would be back to smuggling cigarettes and liquor across the border. Granted, the money was sensational, certainly more than he had been making at his previous job, and the danger involved, though minimal, was a stimulant. The image of an outlaw seemed to appeal to Paul. Of course, there was also the career he was planning in rap music. He wrote his own lyrics, telling anyone who would listen that he was going to be the next Vanilla Ice.

The nearest Karla would come to being a veterinarian was working for one. She enjoyed the job, but never made the push to furthering her education. Helping out around the office was quite taxing enough for the pampered princess.

Nothing much was expected from Karla; she played the "dumb blond" role to the hilt. She had learned long ago that if people thought you were not very smart, they expected less from you, which saved you a lot of work. She also realized that when a person was considered ditzy and not very bright, people let their guard down. They trusted you more and were easier to manipulate because they never expected it, especially if you let them believe what you wanted from them was actually their idea.

It was simple psychology and so far it had worked. Karla allowed Paul to believe he called the shots, that he was the one in control, never realizing that he was playing right into Karla's hand.

She would have pitied him really, if she had not despised him so much.

Sometimes the role of the doting, wide-eyed waif bored her to tears and made her want to retch, but it was getting her what she wanted, so she did her best to suppress those feelings. Karla had wanted the diamond ring, nice house, and expensive car, and she was well on her way to getting everything she wanted.

Paul truly thought she feared him when he threw his temper tantrums. He had gotten physical with her a time or two, but for the most part you just had to ride it out and wait for his mood to improve. Karla had a quick temper herself and even goaded him at times. She let people think he was the bad guy and she was terrified of him because it suited her purpose. Sometimes she liked the brief violent physical encounters their arguments preceded.

Regardless of the reasons why, Karla desperately wanted to hang onto Paul. Be it that she wanted to call the shots, and it was over only when she decided it was over, or if failure in the relationship would damage her pride and ego and cause her to feel rejected, she was willing to go to any lengths to keep him. As their relationship evolved, Paul revealed more of his dark fantasies and evil deeds, and Karla told him she wanted to be a part of them.

Paul's attraction to girls who were petite, with small breasts and a more prepubescent look could have been caused by pedophilic desires alone, or simply a desire to have someone sexually who was untouched by anyone else. He repeatedly stated it was virgins he was most interested in possessing and raping. That was allegedly most of the allure of Tammy. She looked so much like Karla, but she was pure and undefiled.

Later choosing to abduct young schoolgirls, such as Leslie Mahaffy and Kristen French was due to this desire. He quizzed them regarding what sexual experience they had and wanted them even more once he felt he had acquired virgins for himself. What Paul didn't know at the time was that neither girl was a virgin. Both Leslie Mahaffy and Kristen French had boyfriends, and both had already lost their virginity.

Oddly enough, Kenneth Bernardo didn't share any biological link with Paul, who had grown up thinking he was his biological son; yet they both shared a disturbing attraction to young girls. Was this some horrible perverse proof of the nature versus nurture argument or just coincidence? If it was coincidence, an even stranger coincidence was the day both Bernardos were scheduled to appear in the same courtroom. The elder Bernardo was in court to answer charges regarding sexual crimes his daughter he had abused for years said he was now committing on her daughter, and the younger Bernardo was in court to answer to charges for sexually assaulting underage girls.

FIVE

A Bit of Karla

"*It was so gross,*" *Karla had cackled into the phone, as she related the story of the first night she had spent with Paul Bernardo. "I was totally blitzed and the room was so dark, I didn't even realize his poor little pecker was uncircumcised!" Laughing, she went on to say she had given his manhood a nickname. "I call it Snuffles. For some reason it makes me think of Mr. Snuffleupagus." Tears streamed down her face as she howled louder.*

Winding up the phone call, Karla had rolled over onto her back and thought about Paul. At first glance, he had seemed like everything a girl could hope for, and her parents adored him. They were not aware of his dark side, obviously. The darkness that drew her to him like a moth to a flame, was the reason Karla knew they were destined to be together.

She could share her most wicked and perverse thoughts and fantasies with him. Where others had always described the fantasies as "sick" and "disgusting" on the rare occasions Karla had shared them, Paul was not only turned on by them, but his fantasies were even more twisted. This was not just "kinky sex" the couple was talking about, it was brutal, bloody, and possessive.

The idea of choosing a victim together and doing whatever they wanted, truly possessing them and having the power to decide whether they lived or died, was a high. If the visions she dreamed up were this amazing, then the actual acts themselves were going to be pure ecstasy. The power, the control, that's what Karla got off on. (CI)

Karla Leanne Homolka was born to Karel and Dorothy Homolka on May 4, 1970, in Port Credit, Ontario, Canada. Blond, vivacious, and always wanting to be the center of attention, photos depict a smiling, happy child surrounded by friends, but Karla didn't always make friends easily. Bullying others into spending time with her, and dictating what they played and how they played it displayed Karla's need to be in control of herself and others.

Karla learned at an early age that how she acted towards others in individual circumstances allowed her to have the upper hand and control. Karla always had the upper hand. If needed, she could evoke sympathy from a teacher for a low grade, insinuating it was because she was so sickly and frail due to recurring asthma attacks and hospitalizations. She thrived as the master manipulator. If her father tried to intervene on plans Karla had that he didn't agree with, Karla would become vindictive and defiant, causing her father to cave.

Would that talent be used on her future husband, or on their victims?

A story illustrating Karla's love for animals from an early age has often been repeated. Upon finding two boys tormenting a beetle, Karla had rebuked them; stating it was horrible to harm another creature. The story does not include an incident that occurred later in which Karla dropped a friend's hamster from a window to see what would happen`, and then dug up its corpse to view the decomposition.

Whether delighting in the shock and upset the event caused others, or out of genuine curiosity, there is little doubt that Karla's life had taken a decidedly dark turn. The hamster incident is reminiscent of other serial killers, such as Jeffrey Dahmer, who, during childhood and adolescence, also took great interest in the anatomy and decomposition of animals. Although this type of curiosity is not necessarily indicative of a predilection for torturing and killing other living creatures, it should perhaps be noted that both Homolka and Dahmer went on to do just that.

Close to both her younger sisters, Lori and Tammy, all three girls often ganged up on their father calling him a "dumb Czech" and telling him to "fuck off" when they didn't get their way. Karla's friends were stunned at first, but then seemed to brush the behavior aside. Karla was never one to hold back and was always willing to fight for what she wanted.

One of the main things Karla wanted was a boyfriend. The perky blonde had gone through many makeovers and reinventions of herself. She loved shock value, and one way of achieving that in the small town she grew up in was by dressing to match the way she felt on the inside: dark. Gone was the bubblegum-flavored lip gloss and pastel pink nail polish. In their place, Karla painted her nails black, lips blood red, and dressed head to toe in black.

This latest incarnation was also into the occult; devouring books on ritual childhood abuse, Satanism, and witchcraft. Carving symbols into her skin and painting them with black nail polish was more than likely just part of the show she put on as she expounded on the beauty of death. She would tell her friends that death was to be embraced, yet she was obviously focused on life as she plotted and schemed to find a boy. No, a man; a man with money, who would worship her and lavish her with gifts.

But before she could find the man she wanted, she settled for the boy who was available. Shortly after celebrating her seventeenth birthday, Karla followed the boy she was seeing to Kansas, where he had moved with his family. She had sensed she was losing him as the phone calls and letters came less and less frequently. Unwilling to let him go that easily, Karla hopped a flight and stayed two weeks, losing her virginity to him during that time. Although she told her friends she had participated in orgies and BDSM sessions on the trip, the boy denied it, as she also did years later.

Back in Canada and on the prowl once again, Karla took a job working in a pet store at a local mall. The manager quickly struck up a friendship with the teen and even hired one of Karla's closest friends upon her suggestion. Working with animals and one of her girlfriends was like a dream come true for Karla. When their manager took the two girls along on a trip to a work convention and Karla met Paul Bernardo, she felt she had finally met the man of her dreams; her Prince Charming.

SIX

A Bit of Paul

"*S*hit," *he muttered under his breath, as he tried to put the trunk of the large tree between him and the policeman looking in his direction. He knew better than to attempt this, really, he did, but it had become a compulsion almost too strong to fight. Backing away from the tree, never taking his eyes off the officer, he tried to discern whether the cop had actually spotted him or not. Screw it.*

With as casual an air as he was able to muster, he began walking down the sidewalk, away from the bus station, away from the cop, away from the stupid bitch who had made a fuss when she had seen him watching her. This had been a good hunting ground in the past, but now word was travelling about a rapist in the area.

Women were being more cautious, walking in groups to the buses or not taking buses at all anymore.

Knowing that the slim woman with a pinched face was going to kick up a fuss and tell the officer about him, he increased his pace, blending into the crowd a couple of blocks down. Unlocking the door of his small sports car, he slid into the driver's seat and began beating on the steering wheel. "Fuck! Fuck! Fuck!" he yelled into the cold emptiness surrounding him.

Staring at his reflection in the rearview mirror, he saw the sweat dripping down his temples despite the cold temperature. His face was a chalky white instead of a healthy bronze, and his eyes looked terror stricken. He began a mental pep talk; reminding himself to calm down, panicking never got you anywhere except a dank cell that smelled of piss at the police station.

The remedy for his jangled nerves and anger was simple: choose another victim right away. He pulled a list of neighborhoods from his pocket with dates beside them; places and times he had already hit. The important thing was to never hit the same area too frequently because the cops were sure to be staking it out. "Okay, Paul, let's do this," he said to the reflection staring back at him. (CI)

Paul Bernardo's family was as dysfunctional as any found on a late 80's/early 90's American TV sitcom, but very little humor could be found in their story. Paul and his sister were both victims of their father's brutality, or to be more technical, Paul's

43

stepfather. Paul's mother had told him he was illegitimate and the man he grew up knowing as his father never let him forget it.

His sister was being raped and abused by their father on a regular basis. Evenings would begin with their father having too much to drink and cuddling his daughter under a blanket while the three watched television, and would culminate with their father in his daughter's bedroom. How much Paul knew of the abuse and how that influenced his development is up for debate. His mother chose to escape the reality of what was happening in the home by segregating herself from the rest of the family, living in a room in the basement by herself for years.

Born Paul Kenneth Bernardo on August 27, 1964, in Scarborough, Ontario, Canada, he was given the last name of a man with whom he shared no DNA, but with whom he shared disturbing similarities. The young boy with the dimpled cheeks and sparkling smile might not have known the man he called his father had been arrested for a sex crime in 1975, but the boy scout would go on to be convicted of some of the same sex crimes as his father, and worse. The elder Bernardo was charged with child molestation, and his interest in young girls would be an unfortunate and disturbing trait he shared with Paul.

As Paul developed sexually, he realized the fantasies he had begun harboring were much darker than his contemporaries. Reading books that centered around characters who tortured and enslaved women fed his dark desires. He was rapidly developing a taste for sadism, something several women would learn through the abuse incurred during their brief relationships.

Recently graduated from college, with an entry level position at the well-known accounting firm, Price Waterhouse, the solidly built, tall blond had no trouble getting attention from females. When he met Karla Homolka in 1987, he already had two girlfriends. He wasn't looking for anything serious with the seventeen-year-old, but in Paul, Karla saw what she had been searching for and what she felt she deserved. Karla would certainly come to get, at least part of, what she deserved.

When Paul and Karla began dating in earnest, she still lived with her parents and Paul was making the two hour drive on weekends to see her. Soon, he had charmed the entire Homolka family and was invited to start staying the night as their "weekend son." It wasn't long before Karla started turning up the pressure, trying to get Paul to propose and make their relationship more official, but Paul wasn't entirely sure he wanted Karla to be the only girl in his life, especially after meeting her younger sister, Tammy.

Karla knew Paul wasn't monogamous to her, in fact, he seemed to enjoy making her jealous by telling her about his other conquests, but she couldn't compete with these unknown females. She could compete with her own sister for his affection, however, and often did. Karla was worried the one thing she couldn't give Paul that Tammy could; her virginity.

Desperate to keep her man, Karla assisted Paul with rigging Tammy's windows so that he could crawl in her bedroom while she slept. Paul found in Karla the devoted slave who sat at his feet, basking in his glory, hanging onto his every word and ready to make his wishes come true. The couple hadn't been dating long when Paul asked her what she did think if she found out he was a rapist. Her response was, 'she would think it was cool.'

Not only was Karla turned on by the thought of her boyfriend being a rapist, but she was also turned on by the thought of helping him procure victims. She wasn't just another of Bernardo's victims like she later claimed, she was actively planning and participating. The abduction of Kristen French would be just one example of Karla's complicity, because she planned the entire abduction herself. Their meeting in 1987 might have been some evil form of kismet. They were both manipulative co-dependents blazing down the highway to hell, and everyone in their path would get burned.

SEVEN

Leslie

"*Shhh,*" *the woman's voice whispered in the darkness to the young girl.*

Her abductor had gone through the ritual of bathing her battered body after the latest round of abuse, and the girl was once again placed in a dark closet with a blindfold covering her eyes and blocking out even the small shafts of light that filtered in from the cracks around the closet door.

A teddy bear was thrust into her arms. "Here, hold Bunky," the woman told her. This was supposed to be a pact between the victim and her abductors. As long as she had the teddy bear in her grasp, no physical acts would be committed against her. "You know if Bunky's here, you're safe. Night Night," the voice

whispered to her in the darkness, as her captor kissed the first two
fingers of her right hand and placed them gently on the girl's lips
before closing the closet door.

"You know we can't keep her," she said to the man sprawled
out on their bed, as she crawled up next to him. "She has seen our
faces, I know the blindfold slipped. We can't take any chances."

"What did you have in mind?" her partner asked while
flipping through the television channels.

"I'll use one of the syringes to inject some air bubbles in her
bloodstream," the woman purred, shaking her butt like a cat about
to pounce. She was really warming to the idea. The sooner they got
rid of this one, the sooner they could get a new toy to play with.

"If there is nothing on you wanna watch, let's watch the
tape," she suggested, as she stripped off the t-shirt and panties she
was wearing. "I'll wear those things you like," she said, wiggling
her eyebrows suggestively. As she began to pull on the panties that
had belonged to her dead sister, she could hear their voices
coming from the VCR tape they had just made. The girl who was
currently occupying their closet sobbed as she heard her own voice
coming from the television, crying and begging them to stop. (CI)

At fifteen years of age, Leslie Mahaffy was at that time in her
life what makes many teens, especially girls, feel awkward. With
braces on her teeth, the lanky teenager would never have the
chance to grow into a beautiful woman with straight, white teeth.

49

Her braces would be one of the only ways her dismembered body could be identified.

Born the day after the United States celebrated its bicentennial, on July 5, 1976, in Canada, Leslie's father was an oceanographer and her mother a teacher. The Mahaffy family, which included Leslie's younger brother, Ryan, was a tightknit bunch. As Leslie grew older and began to assert her independence, she would often leave the house without telling anyone where she was going. Even if she was gone a couple days, she always called home to let her family know she was safe.

The first sign that something was wrong and Leslie might not be coming home was the weekend of June 14, 1991. Leslie had attended the wake of a friend who had died in a car accident earlier that week. A group of Leslie's fellow schoolmates was meeting at their usual gathering place in some nearby woods to have a few drinks and talk about the loss of their classmate.

People began to disperse and head to their individual homes around 2 a.m. Leslie knew since she had once again missed curfew, her mother had probably locked her out. This wasn't something Leslie initially worried about; if none of the doors were unlocked, she would crash at a friend's.

Luck was not with Leslie that night. All the doors were locked and the friend she called said she could not crash there. Leslie decided not to wake her mother. Opting to accept a ride from a young man she had met, who happened to be in the neighborhood stealing license plates. When she failed to show for her classmate's funeral the next day, everyone knew something was wrong.

Father's Day fell on June 17 that year and the day came and went without word from Leslie. Her mother filed a report with the police listing her as a runaway on June 18. She had no way of knowing at the time that it was too late to begin a search for her daughter. It would be a recovery mission, not a rescue that brought Leslie home.

Paul had arrived home while Karla was asleep in the early morning hours of June 14th and woken her up, telling her he had brought home a surprise. The surprise was a blindfolded Leslie Mahaffy. Unimpressed, Karla planned on going back to sleep and allowing Paul to have his fun with the teenager. It wasn't the first time Paul had abducted a young girl and brought her home with him unexpectedly. In January he had brought home a teen, and Karla had found him in the act of raping her. When done using her, Bernardo released the girl on a country road. Neither bothering asking her name, and thus she was always referred to by the couple as the "January Girl."

Awakening sometime later, Karla went in search of the two. The first thing to catch her eye was the champagne glasses she had bought for herself and Paul to toast each other with at their upcoming wedding. Karla was livid thinking her husband had brought a stranger into their home and allowed her to drink from *her* glass.

Upon tracking Paul and Leslie down, Karla could see her husband was too excited to take her complaints seriously. He had been having fun with his captive; forcing her to drink to excess the way they had with Tammy.

Tammy. Just the thought of her beautiful, unconscious head cradled in his lap, drove him crazy.

If he could not have Tammy again, he could at least have some of the experiences he'd had with his lovely Tammy. He was getting good at pretending it was actually Tammy he was with when he had sex or received oral sex. Karla thought it was a turn-on for him when she dressed in Tammy's underwear and clothing before performing fellatio on him, but it wasn't the same. Last time, he had held a picture of Tammy and had gazed at it; talking to Tammy as if she were still alive, still with him, instead of this cheap facsimile.

It could never be the same without Tammy, though. He wasn't even attracted enough to Karla to maintain an erection. She tried to make it work, rubbing Tammy's panties up and down his shaft while telling him how much she loved him and enjoyed watching him rape Tammy. She wanted to do it again, she said. She wanted to do anything that would make him happy.

With that in mind, Bernardo directed Karla to begin the sexual assault on the still blindfolded, and now bound, Leslie, while he watched. As he joined in, picturing Tammy in place of Leslie, he and Karla once again took turns filming the acts. Bernardo told Leslie she was doing such a good job, and if she kept it up he would return her home soon. Then he looked directly into the camera lens and shook his head no.

Whoever you choose to believe, spending the night blindfolded and drugged in a dark closet after hours of torture and assault, someone killed Leslie the next day. Karla said Paul strangled the teen to get her out of the way before the couple's family came over to celebrate Father's Day.

Paul, of course, pointed the finger at Karla. Karla, known to be jealous of other girls, was already mad about Paul sharing champagne with Leslie and drinking from the couple's "special" glasses. It is entirely possible — it has even been speculated that Karla committed all the murders, including Tammy's. In some people's opinion, Karla had enough knowledge about the drugs she used and resuscitation techniques that Tammy's death was no accident. Karla's jealousy might have boiled over the night of Tammy's death and the master manipulator was able to eliminate what she considered her greatest competition, even convincing Paul it was a terrible accident.

What is known for certain. The body of Leslie Mahaffy was wrapped in a blanket and carried by the couple down to a small, cool room with a dirt floor in a corner of the basement. Leslie's broken and brutalized body would spend the night there while they decided how to dispose of her after Paul and Karla hosted the Father's Day family dinner. The only time Karla broke a sweat was when her mother offered to go down to the basement and bring up potatoes for the meal. Karla declined, telling her mother to sit and rest.

After the family left, the couple tackled the problem of what to do with Leslie's remains. They decided on buying several bags of concrete mix. They then erected a small enclosure in the basement out of tarps. Using a circular saw his grandfather had given him, Paul dismembered Leslie's body within the confines of the makeshift plastic tent. The tent minimizing the need to scrub blood, bone, and tissue off the walls. The concrete was mixed and used to hide body pieces small enough to easily carry out of the home, undetected.

Paul testified at trial that although he did the dismemberment, he would hand Karla the body part he had just hacked off and she would carry it over to the basement sink. He worked methodically, removing Leslie's head from her torso, then sawing off all four limbs, which he further cut into two pieces each. The parts were then parceled up, except the torso, and encased in 2x2x1 blocks of concrete, which they had planned on dumping in a local waterway. Although Paul testified that he alone, without Karla, removed the concrete blocks from the home, the sheer size and weight of the finished concrete seems to dispute his testimony.

The day the blocks were discovered, June 29, 1991, Bernardo and Homolka were getting married.

It was warm and sunny, and several of the locals were out enjoying the beautiful weather, fishing and boating. One man and his wife noticed as they launched their canoe that there were black-colored square blocks that were obviously not organic in nature. While carrying their boat down to the water, he had accidentally stepped on the top of one and the top broke off. What he glimpsed inside could not possibly be what it looked like, he told himself.

Returning to the shore later in the day, the man asked another gentleman and his son, who were fishing from the shore, if they had noticed the blocks. As the small group of people crowded around the items in question, any doubt the man had was quickly wiped away. There, surrounded by concrete, were a foot and lower leg of what turned out to be a young female.

Her torso would be discovered the following day when it snagged on a fishing line.

While post-mortem reconstruction and exams were being performed, the newlyweds honeymooned in Hawaii, their ever present video camera in tow to capture every moment. From the footage they took, if they had any concerns about being linked to the murder of Leslie Mahaffy, they certainly didn't show it. Paul would say later that he had hoped the body wouldn't be discovered so soon, but he had done what he could at the time to cover their tracks.

The body parts were rinsed off before being placed in green garbage bags and then dropped into what a witness who discovered the remains described as "concrete coffins." These parcels of concrete were then painted black and loaded up for the trip to their watery grave. Another witness at the scene, when Leslie's remains were found, said whoever killed and dumped the girl must not be a local. Any local would have known that only a few hundred yards further down the unpaved road, the blocks could have been pushed directly from the vehicle into the water, as opposed to lugging them by hand down to the shore.

It is interesting to note that as the couple boarded a plane to Canada, a Honolulu newspaper ran a front page story about the abduction and rape of a local woman. A copy of one of these papers dated July 11, 1991, with the headline, "Pulled off road and raped says woman in Maui" was found among the couple's possessions during a later search of their home.

Coincidence? Maybe. As calculating as the couple, who were known to keep trophies of their victims, and as addicted as they both seemed to the rush in the abduction and assaults, it is hard to imagine they would take a break just because they were honeymooning.

EIGHT

Kristen

*N*o way was anything going to ruin her mood today.

With school out of the way, her mind was focused on two things; her boyfriend, Elton, and her upcoming sixteenth birthday. She had told her parents that she would make a list of gift ideas.

Elton was sure to get her anything she asked for. He was so thoughtful and always gifting her with things to make her feel special. She thought Elton was special, too. The solidly-built hockey player towered over his fifteen-year-old girlfriend, but he was a big softy when it came to her.

The only complaint, if she had any, was that Elton was no dancer. She had begged her parents that morning to allow her to *go to a local dance club, even though it was a school night. As long as Elton took her, they were fine with it.*

Well, she sighed to herself, it was all right if she didn't get to dance, her leg and back were killing her anyway. She had learned to deal with a lot of pain in her short life, and dancing or no dancing, pain or not, she would have fun. 'Life is too short.' She had no idea how true that sentiment would be in her case. (CI)

Kristen Dawn French was born May 10, 1976, in St. Catherine's, Ontario, Canada, to parents Doug and Donna French. The parents doted on their spunky, brunette beauty. Kristen was noted for her ever-present smile, willingness to help others, and sheer grit and determination.

Kristen had given up the competitive skating she had once enjoyed in favor of being on her school's rowing team. She struggled, with very little complaint, with a condition which left one of her legs shorter than the other, causing pain, numbness, and some difficulty ambulating. Kristen was not one to wallow in self-pity. She did not expect or desire sympathy, nor special treatment.

In 1991, the fifteen-year-old was embracing life and its challenges with the same gusto and energy she brought to everything. She was soon to start a new job shampooing client's hair for a local business and was excited by the prospect. Kristen was known to be extremely responsible, often babysitting for neighbors, and she rarely varied her routine, or her route to and from school.

Her parents knew that generally by 3 p.m., their daughter would have arrived home via the route she always took from school, ready to let her dog, Sasha, out for some play time and food. If anything occurred that would cause Kristen to deviate from her plans, she could be relied upon to let her parents know something had come up. In the days before everyone carried a cellphone, Kristen was aware of the need to let others know where you were at all times. Safety was something her family had not worried about much, but Kristen was their baby, so of course they worried. Especially when they arrived home and saw Sasha was still in her kennel.

Kristen's father set out looking for her, stopping by her school and then driving down the route he knew his daughter usually took. Her mother was busy calling her friends, frantic to find out where Kristen was last seen and when. The worried parents had no way of knowing that it was the kindness and desire of their daughter to help others that two cold-blooded killers would prey upon.

Karla and Paul had formulated a plan to snag their next victim. Karla would stand near a busy thoroughfare with map in hand, as if lost and looking for directions. No one would be suspicious of a young woman, especially with so many potential witnesses and traffic surrounding her. Witnesses would indeed see Kristen French's abduction, but descriptions given to the police were of two males, and the color, make, and model of car had been completely wrong.

Karla pushed the young girl into Paul's car and sat in the backseat, her fist gripped tightly around Kristen's beautiful brown hair. Brandishing a knife, Paul warned her not to fight or make any noise unless she wanted her throat cut. Making the easy drive to the home they had purchased shortly before Leslie Mahaffy's abduction and murder, Karla sped into the house and unplugged all phones, except one. If either of the two received a call, which went un-returned for too long, someone might get suspicious. The couple was learning from prior mistakes they had made, and were getting better with each subsequent abduction.

One of the things Kristen might have worried about, was that she had seen the faces of her abductors. Rarely do kidnappers let a victim live, who would be able to identify them. It was only after they had pulled into the garage that she was blindfolded. Like Leslie Mahaffy, Kristen French might not know how to lead the police to the house she had been taken to, but she knew her captors faces. This leaves little doubt that the two had no plans to let Kristen go.

While Karla busied herself in the kitchen making dinner, Paul began his assault on Kristen; once again filming the entire time. Paul had given Kristen a mixed drink to sip, hoping to calm her down. Kristen promptly vomited up the alcohol, apologizing to her captors for inconveniencing them by being sick. Karla cleaned the girl up. Paul gave her a couple pills to put her to sleep, and she was then placed in their bedroom closet for the night. The Bernardo and Homolka crimes were starting to fall into set patterns.

During Kristen's captivity, Paul forced her to tell him how lucky his wife was to have him and that all her fellow classmates thought he was hot and wanted to have sex with him. Kristen's strategy for survival, doing what she was told, being polite, and trying to avoid anything that might upset her captors, probably did serve to extend her life. By the next night, Paul and Karla felt comfortable enough that Kristen would not try to escape that they allowed her to sleep in their bed.

The length of time Kristen French was held captive was never determined. Through video footage the couple took, as well as their testimony to authorities, it is known she was held at least over the weekend, with some estimates stating she was held for a couple weeks. After the first night of rape and abuse, Paul and Karla settled on a sick game to play with the teen.

Karla, always sensitive to the fact she was no longer as young and trim as she had been when she had met Paul, dug through her old clothes. Finding what she was looking for, she dressed as closely as possible to the Catholic school girl uniform Kristen was wearing when they had abducted. The skirt was now too small in the waist, but Karla's ego convinced her she was a knockout and could easily pass for one of Kristen's classmates.

Playing off Paul's instructions to do stuff average girls do for the camera, Karla and Kristen primped and preened, Kristen, following the older woman's lead and trying to pretend they were friends just hanging out. More abuse followed, again caught on camera, before the couple announced that the theme should continue with fast food and movies. Leaving Karla to guard Kristen in his absence, Paul went to rent movies and pick up food, having told Kristen she could have anything she wanted to eat.

This game, making the victim feel as if they are accepted as a peer by their abuser, is particularly repugnant. Giving a captive the glimmer of hope that things will turn out all right, and the abuse will stop and they will be returned safely to their family is a form of psychological terrorism. After spending time alternately assaulting Kristen and then treating her as a friend or houseguest, it could be expected she would feel not only confused, but disheartened as well. Adding to her misery, Karla had wheeled a television set in so Kristen could see a segment of the evening news in which her father cried while voicing his own hope for her safe return.

Paul arrived home to find Kristen in tears and exploded upon finding out Karla had allowed the girl to see the news concerning her abduction. Not only did it remind Kristen she was being held against her will, but it also served to dissuade her from being as polite and compliant as she had been up to that point. It was never really a question if Kristen would be allowed to live, merely how long, but Bernardo felt pressure to end the charade sooner than he had anticipated.

The last words known of Kristen speaking were to Paul, after he had verbally attacked her and committed a particularly vicious sexual assault on her. Prior to that viciousness, Kristen had remained the polite young woman her parents had raised her to be, but at that point, Kristen knew any kind words were lost on the monster and she would never leave the house alive. While Karla continued to film, Kristen told her abuser she did not understand how his wife could stand to be married to him. The tape ends before Kristen finishes what she had to say to the child rapist.

Kristen French's nude body would be found discarded in a ditch less than six hundred yards from the grave of Leslie Mahaffy on April 30, 1992. Her long, brunette locks had been shorn off.

Which one of the sadistic duo had killed her also remains a mystery.

The medical examiner noted a distinctive pattern of bruising on Kristen's body. The same pattern would also be noted on Leslie's body, after it had been exhumed and a more thorough post-mortem exam performed for comparison. Kristen French's injuries were not confined to those bruises. She had fractures of the ribs and extensive, deep tissue bruising of the head and torso. The injuries inflicted to her head were so bad she had developed subdural hematomas.

More than likely, Kristen French would not have survived her injuries. Homolka's claims that she did not kill any of her and Bernardo's victims might be incorrect; even if the resulting death was accidental. When Bernardo left Homolka to guard Kristen on her own while he went to pick up food, he had given Homolka a rubber mallet to use on Kristen if she tried to escape.

When Bernardo returned home, Kristen French might have already been dead or in the process of dying, unbeknownst to her captors.

We will never really know because Bernardo and Homolka pointed the finger at each other for Kristen French's death.

NINE

Dream House Disintegration

*H*e *hated the sight of the pink house now; the one Karla had likened to a Barbie doll house.*

At first, it was cute the way Karla referred to the two of them as Ken and Barbie, but it got old pretty quick. She had dragged her collection of dolls along with her when they moved in, and went berserk when he hid them as a joke after one of their now all too frequent arguments.

Telling her he had thrown them away, he wasn't prepared for her reaction. Scooping up his car keys from the table near the front door, she ran to the kitchen and dropped them down the garbage disposal, flipping the switch on before he could comprehend what was happening.

"Jesus Christ!" he had screamed over the horrible metallic grinding. "It was a joke, you crazy bitch!"

"Really Paul? A joke? A joke like the way you never listen to me and almost got your ass arrested?"

He wanted to ignore the question, end the argument, and focus on how he was going to get a new set of keys from the dealership. He knew Karla was talking about what had happened a few nights before. While she had been sleeping, he had crept out of the house, put his car in neutral and coasted out of the driveway to keep her from waking up when the engine started.

Without any set destination in mind, he had just driven, winding up in a sub-division where he cruised quietly, looking for darkened houses with a light burning in a bedroom. If he was lucky, he could usually find one pretty easily that had enough bushes to keep anyone passing by from seeing him, but enough space to wedge himself between the leafy branches and the house.

Usually, he settled for watching a woman strip down or sleep in the nude while he masturbated. Tonight, though, he happened upon a young woman out walking a toy poodle. He hated dogs. Despite having a dog allergy, he had bought Karla a dog, knowing it was something that would appease her.

He cruised past the woman, pretending not to notice her, so as not to arouse her suspicion about a strange man in a strange car being in her neighborhood in the middle of the night. Cutting the engine, he pulled alongside the curb and got out, leaving the car door open to maintain silence. Creeping slowly up behind her would not work because she had a dog. So he chose instead to run as quickly and as stealthily as possible, grabbing the dog and snapping its neck.

Throwing the dog's body on the pavement, he body-slammed the woman onto the lawn, hoping to knock the breath out of her, preventing her from screaming. As he placed his hand over her mouth however, she clamped down on his fingers, biting so hard that it was he who yelled out. Almost immediately, a light went on in the house in front of them.

Smacking her across the face, he leaped up and sprinted to his car. Speeding off, he looked down at the gas gauge and saw it was almost empty. One of the things Karla had instructed him to do to help cover his tracks was to always have a full tank, and when needing gas, to fill up at the station near the house. Needing to stop in an unfamiliar area for gas would draw attention to him; clerks were sure to remember the stranger if questioned by police, and an errant gas receipt would place him at the scene of the crime. Damn Karla. (CI)

In late 1992, Paul Bernardo was once again brought into the police station and questioned about the Scarborough rapes. Without a doubt, he was aware the net was being drawn closer around him. The wife of one of his closest friends was one of the people who had reported to authorities that they felt Paul was the

Scarborough Rapist. The DNA samples the police had obtained from him had now sat around for almost two years, and unless some miracle occurred and the specimens were lost, the truth would soon come out.

With this knowledge pressing down on him, he and Karla got into a heated argument near the beginning of the new year in 1993, during which he savagely beat her with a flashlight. The blows to the back of the head with the heavy metal flashlight were administered with such force that her brain moved forward, bouncing off the frontal aspect of her skull, ripping and tearing, causing blood to pool in her eye sockets.

Karla returned to work after the Christmas break with two black eyes she was unable to disguise with makeup, telling co-workers she had been involved in a car accident. Karla, also knowing that the police were probably going to arrest Paul for the Scarborough attacks and eventually discover the link to the Mahaffy and French crimes, assented to being examined and treated at the local hospital. She also filed assault charges against Bernardo.

Karla was admitted to the hospital. Tests were performed, and she was kept under medical observation. Playing on the battered spouse theme, Karla claimed she now feared for her life. She also hinted she knew Paul was capable of taking a life and this time it might be hers.

Upon discharge, she opted not to return to the home she shared with Bernardo. The obvious reason being she wanted to be nowhere near her husband, but also because ever since the murders of Leslie Mahaffy and Kristen French, she had felt uncomfortable in the house. She was convinced the ghosts of the two girls were in the house and would never allow her any peace.

If the hauntings were real, they were justified. Karla did not deserve a moment's peace after the crimes she had helped perpetrate. So convinced she was that the house was haunted, she spoke with a woman claiming to have psychic abilities. The woman said she detected a female spirit, who was angry because she had been hurt and assaulted, felt trapped in the house and not at rest in the residence. She got the sense this female spirit hated Paul in particular. Her recommendation? Pour ammonia down the drains, and carry an amethyst to protect her from the angry spirit's wrath.

Karla confessed to her mother what had happened the night Tammy died. Dorothy told her daughter she was not surprised; she'd had a feeling Paul was involved. Karla also called her aunt and uncle, and told them of her involvement in the deaths of her sister, Tammy, Leslie Mahaffy, and Kristen French, as well as details of crimes committed by Bernardo on his own.

Ever the self-preservationist, Karla's next move was to line up a defense lawyer. After telling the defense attorney her gruesome story, they formulated a plan to keep her out of prison, if possible. Karla and her lawyer met with a psychiatrist, who listened to her story and claim to being a victim of Paul Bernardo as well. A battered woman, in fear for her life. The doctor was more than willing to believe Karla's tale of martyrdom.

Karla was admitted to a psychiatric facility so she could be treated for depression, anxiety, and mental health issues caused by the suffering she had allegedly experienced at the hands of her husband. Karla went through the motions of playing the victim of mental, physical, and emotional abuse who no longer wanted to live. Karla's voracious appetite for reading would pay off.

Years earlier, Karla had read a book called, *Michelle Remembers*, carrying the tome and repeatedly reading its text, until the pages were worn and dog-eared. The story, reputedly based on actual events, was about a girl who was the victim of satanic ritual abuse, and the devastating effect on her mental and emotional health in a time before the term "PTSD" was well-known. In her interaction with hospital staff, law enforcement, and attorneys, Karla appeared to take cues from the title character of the book. She began affecting a way of speaking in a small, child-like voice, while expressing fears associated with those who suffered great abuse, as she clutched her teddy.

Laying groundwork for a defense was one strategy, but it would be even better if a defense was not entirely necessary. The way to accomplish this, and avoid being tried as a co-defendant beside Bernardo, was to approach authorities with the intention of signing a plea bargain. Karla would confess to her part in the crimes, and give them information needed to put Bernardo away for the Scarborough rapes, and the murders of Tammy Homolka, Leslie Mahaffy, and Kristen French.

Karla's excuse that she had only participated in crimes out of her fear of Bernardo, would only hold up provided no evidence was discovered of her being a willing and compliant partner in crime. If the tapes she and Paul had made of the rapes were found, it would be difficult for her to prove she was acting out of fear. When Karla left Paul in early 1993, her parents, who had come by to help her get what she needed from the house, found her searching in vain for something in an upper area of the garage. It was later revealed that area had been where she and Paul had hidden the tapes. Maybe Paul realized he could not trust Karla and had moved the tapes without telling her.

Karla knew there was evidence that would disprove the battered wife scenario, and the important thing to do was get the plea bargain wrapped up before the truth came out. If she could pin the murders on Paul, the charges of kidnapping and assault would deliver much shorter sentences. Karla had sold her soul, and she was about to sell Bernardo up the river in what would come to be called the Crown's "deal with the devil."

TEN

Deal with the Devil

Karla's defense attorney, George Walker, was having difficulty reconciling the image of a battered wife with the crimes his client had admitted to, in private, taking part in.

No one could possibly make up a story like this, though. With mixed feelings and a sense of foreboding, the attorney approached the Crown's prosecution with an offer.

Karla would provide enough evidence to put Paul away for the Scarborough rapes, the murders of Tammy Homolka, Leslie Mahaffy, and Kristen French in exchange for complete immunity.

Prosecutor, Murray Segal, director of the Crown's law office in St. Catherine's, laughed at the defense lawyer's request for blanket immunity. Saying he was being asked to "buy a pig in a poke."

The prosecution could not take the chance of accepting such an agreement only to find out there was insufficient evidence. Law enforcement had been working hard to solve the dozens of rapes, multiple disappearances, and murders in their area. It was risky to make a deal on little information.

One of the problems Segal was concerned with was whether he had the authority to offer and approve a deal. It depended on what crimes they were talking about. Depending on where the crimes had taken place, they might not even fall within his jurisdiction. George Walker made the decision to outline, for Segal, what crimes his client would plea to having knowledge of and been witness to; namely the deaths of Tammy Homolka, Leslie Mahaffy, and Kristen French.

Karla had been adamant that, although she had been present when the girls died, she had nothing to do with the actual deaths — it was all Paul. To be quite honest, Walker was not sure he entirely believed everything his client said, but it was not his place to figure that out. It was his job to get the best possible outcome for his client, no matter her guilt or innocence.

One of the concerns by both defendants was media coverage of the trials, and how that might influence the verdict and sentencing. With Karla opting to strike a plea agreement and wave her right to a trial by jury, media coverage would affect her on a lesser degree. Meanwhile, Bernardo and his lawyers would have to worry about the possibility of a jury holding his fate in their hands. A jury who had been privy to all the lurid details of the crimes in the media. The prosecution certainly did not want to take a chance on a mistrial declared due to a jury biased by news stories.

In the end, it was decided a gag order and publication ban would be enacted. The press; the few who could squeeze in to the fewer than one hundred seats not occupied in the courtroom, would only be allowed to listen to the proceedings. They were forbidden from writing about any aspect of either trial. Such a tight lid was being kept on information that the media was not aware if Karla had pled guilty or not guilty.

The same rules did not apply to American journalists. The few allowed to be present at the defendants' trials could not be forced to refrain from printing the testimony they heard. Thus, the Canadian government also put a ban in place on any American newspapers being brought into the country for sale. Canadian news vendors were not permitted to accept any newspapers from the U.S. for sale. Anyone attempting to cross the border with more than one copy of any American newspaper had to relinquish their copies to be destroyed.

In a time of "big brother" and social media, where everything is on display and it seems there is very little privacy left, this is hard to imagine. How do you keep an entire country ignorant to such a huge news story? The only country which seems capable of doing that today is North Korea.

Once Karla had neatly sewn up a plea agreement she was satisfied with, going so far as to tell a friend that she might be out of prison in only four years, she was more than willing to talk. She gave prosecutors all they needed to convict Paul Bernardo. Authorities had found a home movie that was to become known as the "Karla Sex Tape." Although some scenes were of Karla Homolka and Bernardo, there were scenes that included young women, who Karla was committing sex acts on. Several were obviously willing partners, such as a prostitute Paul and Karla had picked up and brought back to their hotel room in Atlantic City. When the woman was tracked down, she admitted to having sex with Karla, but had no idea the acts had been filmed.

Others, such as a young girl identified in court documents only as "Jane Doe," were quite obviously unconscious during the filming. When officers viewed the tape, they had no idea at first who the victim was, how to find her, or if she was even alive. Watching the footage countless times, some clues emerged and known victims of the couple were excluded as possibilities of being the girl in the video.

The unconscious girl was shown briefly and only from the chest down. Using the small amount of evidence they had, the officers ruled out Tammy Homolka or Leslie Mahaffy from being the girl seen with Karla. Both were blond and Jane Doe was a brunette; judging from the color of her pubic hair. On the tape, Karla takes the lifeless hand of Jane Doe and uses it to penetrate herself. Kristen French was missing the tip of her finger from a childhood accident, so she was excluded as well.

Authorities confronted Karla with still images gleaned from the video footage. Her first comments were that the stills were too blurry for her to make out any details and she could not be sure of when the event had taken place; although she readily admitted it was her in the video. In fact, Karla knew the entire time who the girl was, but she had to prepare for the reveal.

Karla ensured her lawyer had a blanket agreement this time; any evidence or crimes not already known to authorities, even if Karla was involved, would not be used against her in either a future trial or alter the terms of her current plea agreement. She could tell them anything now. Paul had considered himself untouchable at one time, but Karla was proving not necessarily untouchable, as much as touched by luck.

The story Karla would tell about the identity of Jane Doe and how she fit into the picture was another example of the couple's depravity. Jane, as the victim will continue to be called here, was a fifteen-year-old Karla had met a few years earlier, when she still worked at the pet store. Jane would come by to play with the puppies. She was a sweet, helpful child, always delighted to do small chores around the shop.

Karla decided that Jane would make the perfect wedding present for Paul. She had gifted him her sister, Tammy, for Christmas, and now, with their wedding a short time off, she would gift him Jane. Jane's mother thought it odd, initially, when her daughter told her Karla had invited her over to see her new house and the puppy Paul had given her, but was ultimately persuaded.

Jane loved puppies so much and Karla had been so good with Jane in the past, and when Jane's mother found out it was to be a girl's night, as Paul was out of town, it seemed safe enough. Jane was ecstatic and had a hard time controlling her excitement, but there was no need to stifle her girlish delight. Around someone as young as Jane, Karla became a contemporary; giggling and acting just as silly as the fifteen-year-old.

After playing with the puppy, touring the house, having dinner at a nearby restaurant, and watching a movie, Jane was getting tired, but Karla had another surprise in store. Jane had always wanted to try alcohol, but never had the opportunity; Karla was about to provide her that opportunity. Serving Jane mixed drinks with some crushed Halothane added, Jane was soon passed out cold. Karla called Paul, who was out. He took the call on his car phone. He needed to come home right away; Karla had a surprise.

Karla had procured more Halothane from work, and although she wanted to repeat for Paul what had taken place with Tammy, she wanted to ensure Jane did not suffer the same fate as Tammy. She used the Halothane to keep Jane sedated, but monitored her extremely closely. After raping Jane and committing the act authorities had seen on the video, Jane was put to bed. She woke up feeling nauseous, but otherwise okay.

The couple, confidence boosted by the successful drugging and raping, invited Jane over and repeated the sedation. Something went wrong this time. Jane stopped breathing. Karla called 911, but Jane's respirations returned while Karla was on the phone, so she cancelled the ambulance. It was a mistake, she told the dispatcher on the other end of the line. Her friend was fine.

ELEVEN

I Think He Is A Monster

With Karla having immunity from being prosecuted for her role in the drugging and raping of Jane Doe, and December 1990 death of her sister, Tammy, she took the witness stand to testify against Paul.

Paul's defense team could only hope to discredit Karla, or cast doubt on her testimony. The Crown had decided it would not charge Karla for the crimes she had admitted to after the plea agreement had been signed. They would tack two extra years on to her sentence.

Realizing this, Bernardo's defense hoped to plant enough reasonable doubt in the minds of the jury that it had been Karla, and not Paul, who committed the murders. Even if they were able to establish reasonable doubt regarding who killed the girls, their client could still be convicted of murder; but possibly reduce the charges from first to second degree, which carries a lighter sentence. With time served while Paul sat in his cell awaiting trial, there was also a small possibility he could be released after serving the same amount of time Karla had been sentenced.

Before any testimony had been given in Bernardo's trial, however, a video would be shown which the couple had made after Tammy's death. Taken in the same den where Tammy had died, with a fire roaring in the fireplace, it would come to be known as the "Fireside Tape." Unlike the videos containing the couple's victims, which would not be shown to the packed courtroom of spectators, this video would be seen by everyone in attendance.

Audible gasps were heard from the spectators as the tape started with a naked Karla Homolka masturbating with a wine bottle. Although the crowd had been warned of the graphic nature of the tape's content, it was obvious few were prepared for what they were seeing. As the tape went on, no one was prepared for what they would hear, either.

Karla and Paul discussed, in detail, what they had done to Tammy. Karla told Bernardo how much she had loved it, and they should abduct and rape girls as often as possible. Karla was shown performing various sex acts on herself, as well as Bernardo. She went on to tell him they should have children of their own. Lots of children that he could then rape and take their virginity. She wanted to give Paul as many virgins as she could, to rape, because she wanted to keep him happy.

While on the stand, Karla told the court she was guilty of murder, but had been allowed to plead guilty to manslaughter. When asked if anyone assisted her in the murders, she stated that her then husband, Paul Bernardo had, and pointed to him as he sat at the defense table. For a split second, the two looked at each other and maintained awkward eye contact, then Karla continued.

She related how, over time, Paul had dominated every aspect of her life; abusing her if she didn't follow his explicit instructions. From the way she dressed, to where she was allowed to go, and punishing her with degrading and demeaning acts, such as forcing her to eat his excrement. She did not want to do anything to hurt anyone she said, but when asked why she went along with Paul's abducting, raping, and killing of young girls, Karla simply answered, "Paul wanted it."

Karla's parents and surviving sister sat in the courtroom as a show of support for their eldest daughter. When Karla had first gone to prison, Dorothy and Karel had bought their daughter Sesame Street bed linens and a color television for her cell. Noticeably absent from all proceedings were Paul Bernardo's parents. They did not attend any of Paul's hearings.

Leslie Mahaffy's mother, Deborah, was present when the prosecution showed a clip from the video the defendants had made in which Leslie was begging to be set free to go home to her family. Deborah cried as she listened to her daughter's pleas, and Karla confirming it was Leslie she had been talking to. After relating how she insisted Leslie be drugged before Paul killed her so she wouldn't feel any pain, Mrs. Mahaffy was heard to comment facetiously, "How kind of you." Karla went on to say she had felt sick after Leslie's death, and Mrs. Mahaffy said what was probably on most people's minds. "Good!"

Four days of testimony by Karla had passed, interspersed with video footage the couple had made of the crimes. On the fifth day of the trial, after Karla had led listeners through the evolution and decline of her relationship with Bernardo, after telling them how, at first, she had loved him and he had treated her like a princess. She wanted everyone to know how she felt about him now. Before leaving the witness stand, she looked her ex-husband in the eye and told those present, "I think he is a monster." Bernardo responded by mouthing the words, "Fuck you."

The prosecution wound up its nine days of testimony from Karla with her relating the events regarding Kristen French's murder. Karla told them she knew Kristen would have to die because the couple was having Easter dinner with her family, and they could not leave Kristen alone. Karla had showered in preparation for the family meal. She stood with her damp hair dripping as she watched Paul murder Kristen. She then went back into the bathroom and blow dried her hair, put on makeup, and dressed for the trip to her parent's house.

The defense prepared to cross examine Karla with the goal of discrediting her account of things. The way she seemed to minimalize her part in the crimes, public and press alike wondered how the defense would achieve this goal. One of the ways they did this was by chipping away at Karla's claims she had stayed in the abusive marriage and did as she was told out of fear. Why, if she was so fearful, had she not reported the rapes, or the very least the first murder, of her own sister, Tammy, to the authorities, so she could get away from the "monster," before being married to him. By staying with Bernardo through it all she proved she was complicit, they stated.

When Karla left Paul for good, she did not call the police and tell what had transpired, instead, she went shopping, to the movies, to bars. At one bar, she met a man, who she took to bed the next night. The defense reasoned that her actions were not that of someone burdened by guilt, nor someone in fear for her life. By signing the plea agreement, Karla had never been put on trial, but here, at the trial of her ex-husband, Karla was, in essence, on trial herself. She was being taxed with giving an account of her actions, as well as her inactions. Paul Bernardo was very pleased.

The defense questioned how she could go along with Bernardo's desire to rape her little sister. Why didn't she do something? Tell someone, anything. Anything besides assist him in the assault. The defense alleged that she wanted to add a third person to her sexual activity with Paul as much as he himself, did, and her sister was an easy target.

Karla denied this, saying she never would have complied if she knew her sister's safety would be at risk. She stated she thought if she didn't assist Bernardo that he would grab Tammy off the street and rape her. The rape of her sister, she seemed to be telling the court, was inevitable, and her compliance was her way of trying to ensure Tammy's safety. Audible groans and gasps of disbelief followed her statement. No one could believe that she had not done anything to prevent Bernardo from raping her baby sister. The tide of reasonable doubt was beginning to wash up on the shoreline of the defense.

After attacking Karla's character by insinuating if she loved her sister, she would have gone to any length to prevent her being assaulted, the defense moved on to question her assertion she feared for her life. A plethora of cards and love letters she had sent Paul were introduced into evidence and read to the jury. Surely, if she were frightened and miserable, she would not send her husband cards proclaiming her endless love and undying devotion, especially after Tammy's death.

Also read and admitted into evidence were letters she had written to friends professing her love for Paul, and excitement over their upcoming nuptials. An act, Karla said. It had all been an act, because she did not want to admit to anyone how bad things really were and how abusive Paul had become. One of the letters the defense read out loud spoke of the selfishness of her parents; Karel and Dorothy felt the wedding should be postponed since it was too soon after Tammy's funeral.

In the expletive-filled letter, she wrote how angry she was that her parents said they were not able to contribute much financially to the wedding after having paid for Tammy's funeral. Karel had only worked one day since the funeral. "He's wallowing in his own misery and fucking me."

To counter Karla's claims of being "numb" after Tammy's death, and how she really did not want to marry this man she was becoming to view as a monster, the defense read another excerpt. "'And for the real reason we moved out. My parents told Paul and I that they wanted him to stay at the house until the wedding. Then they said they wanted him to go after Tammy died because they needed their privacy. First, they took away half the wedding money, and then they kicked us out. They knew how much we needed to be together, but they didn't care. What assholes!!!'"

The court was again stunned by the callous remarks, which were in direct contrast to the testimony Karla had given regarding her feelings of being in fear.

Bernardo's defense attorney seemed to be easily and effectively peeling back the façade Karla had wanted others to see and revealing the true Karla. His attack was relentless. Why, when Paul came home and announced he had abducted Leslie Mahaffy, had she not left the house or picked up the phone and reported the abduction? She was too frightened, she responded. To which the attorney replied by asking her if she was so frightened, why had she gone upstairs and read a book.

This was a reference to Karla's timeline of events she had given to law enforcement and her attorney. She had said that when she woke and realized Paul must still be downstairs somewhere with Leslie, she had dressed and taken her dog for a walk, then went back up to her bedroom where she finished reading a book and then began reading a second one. Again, she was reminded that at any point she could have called police, but instead, she spent a leisurely day, all the while knowing her husband was assaulting Leslie Mahaffy.

Repeatedly, the lawyer tried to catch Karla off guard, to make her slip and say something she should not or react in a way that proved to the jury she was not the quiet, submissive, battered wife she claimed to be. The lawyer laid out scenarios in which it seemed highly probable it was Karla, and Karla alone, who had murdered Leslie Mahaffy and Kristen French. Her explosive reaction was exactly what he had hoped for.

The trial dragged on for 48 days, with the prosecution calling 85 witnesses to testify before the defense called its first witness; the one people had waited to hear from: Paul Bernardo. He admitted to kidnapping and raping Leslie Mahaffy and Kristen French. He admitted he had taped the sexual assaults on both girls. One thing he was not, however, was a murderer.

Bernardo looked out at the court from where he sat on the witness stand and stated that he knew he had caused pain and sorrow and he should be punished. As the courtroom grew still and silent, hanging on his every word, waiting to hear what he would say next, he simply left it at, "I didn't kill those girls." The inference being that it was Homolka who had committed the murders, or at least one of them. He believed Leslie was smothered with a pillow by Karla, but he had not been around when it had occurred. Kristen, he said, had accidentally strangled to death trying to escape.

The death of both girls, he further stated, was something he thought would bring the couple even closer. After they found Kristen's lifeless body, he said they had held each other and wept. Instead of bringing them closer, though, Bernardo continued, it pushed a wedge between the couple and their marriage fell apart.

The couple's bond had always been sex from the beginning of their relationship, he told the jury. It progressed from what some considered kinky sex, but clearly was the norm for Paul and Karla, such as handcuffs and bondage and then to threesomes. When threesomes seemed to lose some of their thrill, the idea of raping Tammy came up. Both of them were excited by the idea, he testified.

They had enjoyed the rape so much that Paul wanted to continue the mutual pleasure by kidnapping and raping other girls. That's how he had come to abduct Leslie Mahaffy and then

Kristen French. This was for both of them. He had grown particularly fond of and attached to Kristen. He had a desire to keep her with them; the three of them could be in a relationship together. When Kristen died, he took it especially hard. He blamed Karla and beat her for allowing Kristen to die.

It seems surprising that after all the testimony, from witnesses as well as Karla and Paul, and after hearing the tortured screams of their victims, the jury deliberated for eight hours before returning with a verdict. Paul Bernardo was found guilty of all charges. The defendant, knowing this was sure to be the outcome of his trial, accepted the decision without any outward sign of emotion.

He was sentenced to life with possibility of parole after twenty-five years on September 1, 1995.

TWELVE

Aftermath

The Mahaffy and French families fought valiantly to keep videotapes of their loved ones being raped and tortured from being shown to the press and public during the initial trial.

Granted, even the audio being played in court was of such a graphic nature that no one who heard it will ever forget. The video could technically be considered the most disturbing of child pornography. The videos of the assaults played in court were only allowed to be viewed by the presiding judge and jury, both sets of attorneys, and the defendants.

A reporter had filed a motion for, and was granted access, to the sealed records and videotapes under certain "right to know" and "freedom of expression" statutes pertaining to the press. It was later discovered the same reporter had set up a website on which confidential material had been listed naming names and identifiers of other victims of Bernardo's; one victim only fourteen-years-old at the time of the assault. The website was taken down, but it was also brought to the court's attention the reporter had sold a clip of the rape of Tammy Homolka to the media outlet HBO for an undisclosed sum. The burden on the families of wondering if someday a bootleg copy of their loved one's final moments might wind up on the internet, is unimaginable.

The court announced in December 2001 that all known copies of the tapes, which documented the physical and mental torture of not only Leslie Mahaffy and Kristen French, but also Tammy Homolka and the victim referred to as Jane Doe, had been destroyed after being held as evidence for the prescribed amount of time by law for such materials. Other documents of a graphic nature were also destroyed at the time, after being judged not to be needed for future prosecution. The tapes, not available to the authorities before Bernardo's trial, surfaced after it was reported a lawyer of Bernardo's had them in his possession. He turned them over to authorities and was charged with, but later acquitted of, obstruction of justice.

Families of victims in other criminal trials have been further traumatized in the past when files, which were court-ordered to be sealed, have found their way into public view. In a world of 24-hour news available on multiple platforms, it becomes increasingly harder and harder to maintain secrecy and privacy. The internet is flooded with pictures of crime scenes, and autopsies of everyone from J.F.K. to Jon Benet.

"Right to know" laws weren't written to protect victims and their families, so the survivors must remain vigilant regarding the protection of the memories of those they lost. Paul Bernardo has been due for day parole since February 17, 2015, however, each time the convicted killer had an opportunity to apply for parole, the families steel themselves, and prepare victim-impact statements that will keep him behind bars.

For one reason or another, Bernardo has not pursued an attempt at parole. The, now, fifty-three-year-old was brought up on charges of making and concealing a weapon in April 2018. It could be speculated, as it was with the recently deceased infamous convicted killer, Charles Manson, that Bernardo does not want to be released. He might, in fact, fear retribution from victim's families or vigilante justice outside the segregated walls keeping him safe, is a possibility.

The man who has been imprisoned and segregated for two decades, the man who had chosen the alias Paul Jason Teale — a last name also used by ex-wife, Karla, for a time before their subsequent divorce — was scared. (CI)

Canadian prison guards take their duty to protect prisoners and ensure they complete their sentences, seriously. When Paul Bernardo was convicted and sent to prison, it posed a few problems for the Crown; one being how to protect such a high profile prisoner from the other inmates. A "skin beefer" or child rapist/killer is not tolerated by the general prison population any better in Canada than they are elsewhere. That problem led was how to house Bernardo in a segregated environment that was of a higher degree of security than they had ever provided for a prisoner in the past. A new prison cell was constructed for the convict, which was not only segregated but contained extra precautions; a sheet of bulletproof glass covering the front of the cell. People who have seen it likened it to the cell of Hannibal Lector, in *Silence of the Lambs.*

Perhaps the knowledge that child killers are not safe in prison might explain why, when so close to a potential release date, he opted to make a shiv a few months back. It is also possible that constructing and possessing the weapon could have been a strategy to ensure his safety in prison, but also to lessen the chance of being paroled anytime soon. (CI)

There are many people on the outside of those prison walls who hope Paul Bernardo never experiences freedom again, and would not hesitate to extinguish his life, given the chance.

It has been twenty-five years since Bernardo's spouse made her plea agreement, revealing gruesome details that would contribute to his conviction. October 2018 will find Paul Bernardo eligible for full parole. During his May 18, 2018, court appearance via video link regarding the prison shank he had fashioned,

Bernardo requested that the judge set the trial date for the charges sometime between late September and early October, stating, "Your Honor, I have a parole date in October, and I'd like to have the matter handled before that if that's possible."

Karla divorced Paul, married her lawyer's brother, and started a family. She made a brief appearance on a French language television show in Canada after her release. She has resurfaced at infrequent intervals in the news since then. Karla, or her latest incarnation, Leanne Teale Bordelaise, has lived in several different countries over the past few years, including Guadalupe, and as of this writing, is back in Canada once again.

Karla enraged many people over the years, but most notable are the parents of young children in recent years. Karla was outed on a website devoted to mommies and children, when a user realized it was Karla using an alias, dispensing parenting advice and selling her own line of handmade baby clothes. She must have panicked the first time she noticed one of the users, who was on to her real identity, had the username "Kristen French."

Parents at the school Karla's children attended in a Canadian suburb were likewise seething with fury when they found out she was volunteering there. The school, at first, berated the parents and refused to give Karla the boot. Maybe after discussions with their legal advisors, and taking into account a condition of her release was that she have no contact with children, they changed their stance. She was ultimately relieved of her duties.

Justice in the story of Karla Homolka might be that she can never truly live in peace. Whether the spirits haunt her or not, she will never be free from Tammy Homolka, Leslie Mahaffy, or Kristen French. The world knows what she did to those girls and the world will not let her be at peace.

Paul wrote and released a self-published book on Amazon in 2015. Drawing parallels with O.J. Simpson once again, the book was a work of fiction akin to Simpson's, *If I Did It*. Amazon pulled the book from its website following a multitude of indignant complaints from customers.

While Karla seems to have dedicated herself to raising a family, Paul has no children, but made news when it was reported he had gotten engaged while in prison. There has been no evidence the convicted killer married for a second time, but there has been evidence of a different sort.

Since Bernardo's conviction in 1995, evidence has linked him to further rapes, disappearances, and homicides. In at least two cases, innocent men had been convicted and were serving time for crimes Bernardo had committed. Bernardo later confessed to both crimes. The first was the murder of a young woman, whose boyfriend was convicted and sent to prison. The second case was the rape of a fifteen-year-old girl, the average age of Bernardo's rape victims.

While researching this story, I came upon information I had not heard before. I was not aware the reason why Paul and Karla had chosen the last name Teale, was an homage to the killer in a favorite movie of theirs, *Criminal Law*. Karla changed the spelling of the serial killer's name from Thiel, to the phonetic spelling and addition of the letter e.

I was also unaware until researching the characters and their families that Karla's surviving sister, Lori, had also changed her name. More interesting than the name change, however, was the news item that followed. Lori had legally changed her name in 1996, so it came as a surprise when she was contacted by authorities in 2012, asking if she had mailed a package using her birth name on the return address. She has not, of course. Police had a feeling she had not, but had to follow up; the only clue they had at the time as to who might have sent the package containing a human hand.

As it turned out, this was not the only body part mailed, nor was Lori's the only return address to be forged. Another package had the name and address of a former prime minister's son. Police were finally able to track down the murderer; a porn actor named Luka Magnotta, who had dismembered the victim and then mailed some of the body parts.

It is difficult to sum up a story such as this. The two key players are still making headlines on a regular basis. As long as they are alive, and likely even after, their tale will generate interest.

If this had been the plot of a Hollywood movie instead of a true story told through home movies, critics would say this story had it all: sex, murder, romance, mystery, and suspense, plus all the main characters were young and beautiful.

But this isn't Hollywood, and this story, although full of intrigue, is also full of tragedy. The families of the victims will never hold their loved ones again. Never hear their laughter fill the house again. Sadly, it is the memory of the sound of their daughters' cries as they begged their captors to let them live that they hear all too often playing in their mind.

There will never be a satisfactory explanation for why all these things happened. Selfishness and no respect for human life were certainly factors. But the "why" can never be understood, not by those whose lives are dictated by compassion for others and love for their fellow man.

If there is a lesson to be learned here, maybe it is as simple as evil exists, so does good, and it can prevail if we remember those who are lost to us and keep their memory alive. By carrying on the works that were important to them in life, they live on. When we show the love and mercy to others that was denied Tammy Homolka, Leslie Mahaffy, and Kristen French, along with the other victims, they do live on.

Preview of

Robert Berdella

The True Story of a Man Who Turned His Darkest Fantasies into a Reality

(Real Crime by Real Killers Vol 1)

(Second Edition)

Ryan Becker

Introduction

Something must be said: we are fortunate.

We are fortunate because we can sit in the safety of our homes and pick up books like these as a source of entertainment and knowledge, distractions of sorts that allow us to learn the tales of horrible human beings. We are fortunate because as soon as we put these books down, we simply push the horrific details to the back of our minds and or let them remain on the pages of said books. Soon, we forget about them or replace them with more pleasant information.

The victims of the killers we describe, however, are not so fortunate.

Everyone in the world has dreams, desires, and fantasies. While some may wish to travel or possess riches, others may have fantasies of a more intimate nature. There is no real problem with desiring that which you cannot easily have, with wishing for something that may be out of your reach.

Unfortunately, some desires are of the deepest, darkest kind.

A serial killer is described by the Federal Bureau of Investigation as; 'an offender who commits a series of two or more murders in separate events, usually, but not always, acting alone'. Most killers are troubled beings who have suffered traumatic childhoods and cannot live normal, decent lives without causing damage to those around them; others simply enjoy the rush of killing without being discovered. There are many, many more reasons for a human to stray into the act of serial killing, but an even worse category of killer awaits us — one which includes the particular subject of this tale.

Sick individuals have always plagued humanity — monsters that have lost all empathy for their fellow humans and cannot see past their own personal desires. These include: the murderous dictators of recent, as well as those long-dead in the past, the leaders of organizations who have taken lives for perverted or unforgivable reasons such as political or racial preferences, and finally those particular beasts disguised by human flesh that have seen fit to experiment on their own species as if they were cattle.

The subject of this book is one such figure who fits into the latter group.

The press named him *The Butcher of Kansas City*. He was a true psychopath who sadistically tortured and killed at least six men during a three-year period. However, until he confessed and was arrested, our killer was known simply as Robert Berdella.

Robert was a quiet, intelligent fellow who — besides being appreciated by his neighbors as a civic-minded individual — was also a great lover of art, cooking, and different cultures. His activities ranged from hobbies as innocent as stamp collecting to more incriminating pursuits such as possession of illegal drugs and experimentation on animals.

Even so, these particular activities gave no indication for what Berdella would later become. Perhaps one thing led to another, but in truth, it seems more likely that he finally let go of his decency and embraced an evil that had long lingered within his mind.

The murders were ugly events, but it was what Berdella did to his victims *before* death that horrified the entire nation. He experimented on his victims, causing terrible damage to their organs and bodies in general, and usually kept them captive for weeks before they died. Injections of chemical substances, electric shocks, rape, and insertion of objects were just a few of the activities that took place within Berdella's home. It most definitely can be said that The Butcher of Kansas City deserved his nickname.

In the following book, we will relive the tale of this sadistic individual — a man who happily confessed his crimes once caught and talked about having been influenced by *The Collector,* a 1965 movie that allowed him to 'make some of his darkest fantasies become a reality,' as he said at the time.

This book will tell the story of The Butcher of Kansas City from his origins to his end.

Do not believe for one second that the grisly details of Berdella's murders shall be censored or kept from you; these details have been preserved through time thanks to Berdella's own Polaroids and diary. You need to be prepared, beloved reader…

…you're in for a gruesome recount.

ONE

A God-Fearing Boy

Our story begins in Cuyahoga Falls, Ohio, on the 31st of January, 1949. Robert Andrew Berdella, Jr. was born to Robert Sr. and Alice Berdella, a practicing Catholic couple who immediately integrated their new son into their faith. Robert's younger brother, Daniel, was born when Robert was seven, and the two were raised as good, well-behaved boys who avoided bad behavior, lest they anger their strict father.

The young Robert suffered a large amount of bullying during his childhood years due to his nearsightedness that required he wear thick glasses. He slowly turned into a loner who rarely got involved in group activities or social interaction with friends. He was a good student with decent grades, but the constant bullying marred his school years and created a distant boy who behaved in a detached manner

Berdella's teenage years were heavily influenced by his disaffection with Catholicism and a life-changing discovery: he was a homosexual.

When Robert was just 16, his father died of a heart attack at 39 years of age. This caused great sadness in the boy, but nothing hurt him more than when his mother remarried and moved in with another man just a few months later. In Robert's immature mind, this was enough reason to feel insanely angry — he felt as though his mother had flippantly discarded his father's memory and grabbed a new lover instantly while he himself was still grieving.

Initially, Robert attempted to find solace in religion, but this became harder every day, as the pain of losing his father ate away at him. This, along with an incident at work when a male co-worker took advantage and sexually abused Robert, made him reconsider his faith, and he abandoned the Catholic Church for good. He developed a cynical attitude towards religion and he began to read and investigate about different faiths, without truly believing in any of them.

Around the time of his father's death in 1965, Robert watched the film adaptation of the book, *The Collector*. He saw the protagonist capture a beautiful woman, hold her captive in an underground, windowless room, and study her as a sort of specimen. The movie left an impression on the young Berdella, one that was strong enough for him to eventually decide to recreate these events in real life.

Berdella graduated from high school in the summer of 1967. Before long, he moved to Kansas City for a change of scenery. He wanted to study art and become a professor at the Kansas City Art Institute. In college, Berdella was considered to be a talented student who worked extra hard at finding inspiration. However, he worked equally hard at abusing alcohol and he even began to sell minor drugs to addicted classmates. This eventually came back to bite him when he was picked up by the police for possession of drugs. Luckily for Berdella, they lacked sufficient evidence to impose anything harsher than a fine.

Although Berdella had friends in college, he still lacked the mercy that many normal human beings possess. On three particular occasions, Berdella experimented on live animals during art classes; the final time he murdered a dog in front of a crowd 'for art.' The College Board decided that enough was enough. Berdella was stripped of his place at the Kansas City Art Institute; an occurrence that caused him a significant amount of shame.

Where a normal person may have taken this as a signal to turn their life around, Berdella felt aggrieved by his expulsion from the Institute. Surely the Board at the Center of Studies simply didn't understand his brand of art and were *clearly* just repressing his desires. It was at this moment the young Berdella, already troubled, took a turn for the worse. *For the much, much worse, in fact.*

TWO

Berdella's Bizarre Bazaar

During his time studying art, Robert had adopted some unusual pastimes, such as collecting oddities and writing to distant pen pals in countries such as Vietnam and Burma. His interest in primitive art and antiques would eventually drive his desire to open a business in this field, but first, he needed to earn the necessary funds.

Thus, in 1969, following his expulsion from the Kansas City Art Institute, Berdella changed his direction in life. After brief consideration, he decided to move to the Hyde Park district of Kansas City. There, he was a helpful neighbor within the community, taking part in Crime Prevention and Neighborhood Watch patrols, and gaining the love and respect of his fellow Hyde

Park residents. He was also known for participating in fundraising events for a local television station.

Another more secret, yet equally respectable side of Robert's life, was what he did for several vulnerable young men of the city in the early 70s. After having a brief relationship with a Vietnam War veteran, Berdella began spending time with young males who had gotten into prostitution, drugs, or had run away. He tried his hardest to steer these young men back onto the right track and assisting them in leaving their harmful lifestyles behind. Those that were unaware of the sexual nature of some of these relationships thought of Berdella as a sort of 'foster parent' to these young men.

At the same time, Berdella attempted to improve himself on an interpersonal level, while he also strived to enhance his professionalism. Soon he started working as a cook throughout the city. When he wasn't working at a bar or restaurant, Robert found time to sell antique items and art to contacts, all from the comfort of his home. Both of these activities allowed him to succeed and cover his expenses — expenses of which he would soon have many including: lawyer fees and fines that accumulated due to arrests. Berdella eventually became a prestigious, well-known cook in town, working for renowned businesses and even joining a chefs' association where he helped train young students at a local culinary college.

Despite Berdella's success as a cook, however, he found his interest in antiques and oddities couldn't be denied, so he decided to invest the money he'd accumulated in starting an antique-selling business. In 1982, he rented a booth at the Westport Flea Market, naming it *Berdella's Bizarre Bazaar.* He sold jewelry and antiques to both curious amateurs and expert customers.

While managing the booth, Berdella befriended a man named Paul Howell, as well as his son, Jerry. Robert and Jerry soon formed a friendship. They were often seen sharing drinks in the company of friends. At other times, Berdella gave the young troublemaker a bit of legal advice.

To everyone around him, it looked like Robert had finally found someone to care about and spend time with — something he'd never truly had since childhood. What was happening in truth, however, was far more sinister.

Berdella was beginning to measure his first possible victim, a process that would end with bloodcurdling results.

THREE

The Bloodshed Commences

J erry Howell was just 19 when it happened. He'd owed Robert a sum of money for quite a while now and constantly evaded the man's questions whenever the issue came up. As time passed, he seemed less and less likely to pay the debt. This angered Berdella, who was already filled with a strange and misguided anger — just waiting for a reason to unleash it on the world.

It didn't take long to manifest.

On the 4th of July, 1984, Berdella decided that he had waited long enough. The signs had been there for years, but nobody had paid attention. It wasn't really a killing instinct that drove Berdella, but rather the urge to cause pain and push the human body to its extremes. He felt he *needed* to know how much pain he could cause and how much damage and destruction he could inflict on a fellow man.

Berdella arrived at Jerry's home with an excuse already on his lips — he had come to take the young man to a dancing contest. Jerry, naïve of his friend's true motives, got in the car with Berdella. They drove for a while, with Berdella offering Jerry a drink in the car before they reached their destination. Unfortunately for Jerry, the drink was spiked with sedative drugs. Berdella simply drove around killing time until Jerry no longer knew what was happening.

Berdella grew excited and took Jerry back home with him. He injected him with even more tranquilizer to keep him submissive. Berdella bred Chow-Chow dogs and had collected plenty of animal sedatives for when the perfect moment arose. The youth became unconscious and all that Robert Berdella had ever hoped for was now his to enjoy: a helpless victim to torture as he saw fit.

He bound Jerry to his bed with glee, stripping him of his clothes and admiring his body—a body that became the target for more than twenty-four hours of sexual and physical abuse. Berdella didn't just rape Jerry personally during his horrific night of captivity; he also introduced foreign objects — such as a cucumber — into the youth's anus, tearing it without mercy. Whenever Jerry was conscious enough to beg for mercy and ask Berdella why he was doing such terrible things, Berdella would answer with a quick shot of sedative, which put him back under. Berdella even went to work while the man was unconscious, an attempt to keep anyone from suspecting what was truly going on. *His plan worked.*

When he returned from work, Berdella had new ideas how to cause agony to his captive's body. Taking advantage of the young man's helplessness, Berdella continued his torture despite Jerry's pleas for him to stop. The twisted torturer decided to keep mementos for his future pleasure and documented most of the process with his Polaroid camera and a notebook; a pair of items he would soon come to use very often.

The horrific ordeal ended only when young Jerry died sometime after midnight, July 5, 1984. Berdella would later confess that he was unsure whether it had been due to Jerry asphyxiating on his own vomit — he had been gagged for a long period of the torture — or the fact that the excess of medicines had stopped his breathing. After a brief and failed attempt at CPR, a disappointed Berdella lifted up the now dead Jerry Howell and dragged him down to the basement. There, he hung the corpse from the ceiling over a pot and climbed back upstairs to search for his set of cooking knives. Berdella worked on the victim's body like a butcher in a slaughterhouse, cutting open the jugular and inner elbow veins to drain the blood from the corpse.

Berdella left the body hanging overnight, returning the next morning to finish cutting it up with a chainsaw and bone knives. There was a feeling of dissatisfaction growing within him already, but he ignored it long enough to concentrate on disposing of the body in dog food bags that were then wrapped in larger black bags. The bags were left outside for the garbage collectors.

With his first victim dead and a long and detailed document of the killing safely in his Polaroid pictures and diary, another killer may have called it a day.

Berdella, however, was just getting started.

FOUR

\-

New Methods

As we have already mentioned, Robert Berdella enjoyed helping young men get back on their feet during times of hardship. He allowed many of them to stay at his home until they could find jobs and piece their lives back together.

One such lodger was Robert Sheldon, a young man Berdella felt no attraction towards, but who was simply in the wrong place at the wrong time.

On April 10, 1985, Berdella heard a knock at his door. Suspicious, he went to see who had arrived at his home unannounced. Waiting at the door was 23-year-old Sheldon, who needed a place to stay after having been evicted from his own home. Although Berdella agreed to take him in, something stirred within him. It was a mix of discomfort at having someone living in his private space and a curious desire to try out more methods of pain – those he hadn't used in his first murder. He had anger and frustration bubbling within him. *What better way to unleash my feelings than on young Robert?*

So, on April 12, when Berdella arrived home from work to find Sheldon lying unconscious and intoxicated from having drunk too much, he allowed his darker side to manifest. Sheldon was too far gone to feel the needle that punctured his vein. The sedative rapidly spread through his body as Berdella prepared to torture his second victim.

It is interesting to note that, unlike with Jerry Howell, Berdella did not feel any kind of attraction towards Sheldon. This lack of sexual desire led him to avoid inflicting rape or any other type of sexual abuse on the 23-year-old. This did not mean, however, that Berdella was any less brutal in his methods.

He began by binding the young man and leading him up to the second-floor bedroom. There, he began the ordeal by waiting for Sheldon to return to consciousness before explaining what was about to happen to his captive. As the man reeled in shock, Berdella produced a syringe and proceeded to inject Drano (a well-known drain cleaner product) into Sheldon's eyes. Then he grabbed a metal rod and needles, alternating between forcefully smashing his victim's hands and inserting needles into his fingertips.

Berdella used caulking sealant in Sheldon's ears to keep him deaf and unaware of the sounds in his surroundings and raised the television volume to ensure his neighbors wouldn't be alerted by the victim's screams. He also bound Sheldon's wrists with piano wire, a sharp material that cut into the young man's nerves and tendons when he struggled, ensuring that, even if he survived, he'd never be able to use his hands properly again.

It didn't matter in the end

On April 15, three days after the torture began, a workman arrived at Berdella's home. The killer had forgotten he'd scheduled some roof work for that afternoon. Faced with discovery, Berdella quickly but reluctantly went up to the second floor, put a thick sack over Sheldon's head, and pulled a rope tight around the man's neck until he suffocated.

With Sheldon now dead, Berdella allowed the worker to enter his home. Once the worker had left, Berdella dragged the corpse to the third-floor bathroom and dissected it in the tub. Apart from Sheldon's head, he disposed of the corpse similarly to how he'd gotten rid of Howell. Then he sat down to read his notes and inspect his Polaroids. He had 'learned' plenty from both torture-murders. The pain he'd caused Sheldon had been quite intense, despite the fact that he'd left some of his plans unfinished, due to the workman's interruption.

When night fell, Robert went out to the backyard with his victim's head. He buried it for safekeeping — similarly to the souvenirs he had at the Bizarre Bazaar —until when he would relocate it to a closet inside. Nobody had a clue.

Berdella was pretty sure of himself. *I could stop right now.* However, everything had been so easy, with nobody having any inkling of what he'd been doing. *Why stop, if nobody can catch me?*

Ultimately, this was what kept Berdella going — the fact that his victims' disappearances did not register or cause doubts within the community or among law enforcement. It was as if there were no consequences at all for what he had done. It felt as if he could keep going forever if he wanted to, and subsequently he decided to continue killing.

To the misfortune of his victims, Berdella now felt *unstoppable*.

FIVE

Hungry for More

June came and with it, a new victim. Berdella had often hired the services of a youth named Mark Wallace, who did yard work in exchange for a bit of cash.

On one particular afternoon, as a severe thunderstorm raged overhead, Berdella looked out his window and spotted someone hiding in his shed. Squinting his eyes as he approached, he caught sight of Mark Wallace sheltering from the rain in there. Berdella was pleasant as always, calling the young man over and inviting him inside. While Mark believed that his employer's intentions were good, Berdella had already made up his mind.

Wallace would become his next victim.

As thunder and lightning tore through the sky outside, the two talked. Berdella noted the young man sitting across from him was feeling depressed and anxious. He offered him an injection of drugs, saying they would help him feel better and more relaxed. Mark was happy to accept. Berdella got a syringe full of chlorpromazine (a mild sedative) and injected it into the youth.

Unknowingly, Mark had just been manipulated into the worst situation he'd ever face.

Half an hour later, Berdella was carrying the unconscious Wallace up to the second-floor bedroom. Again, he waited for the young man to wake before commencing an entire day of pain and torture.

Berdella had recently been contemplating the effects of electrical shocks on the human body. He now had the chance to find out.

After attaching alligator clips to Wallace's nipples, he kept the youth awake and alert by shocking him whenever he seemed about to lose consciousness. He took photos and documented everything he did, eventually deciding to insert hypodermic needles into the young man's muscles. Berdella enjoyed the torture until Wallace suddenly stopped responding at 7 P.M., June 23. He was dead.

Berdella cursed his luck and took the corpse to the bathroom upstairs, repeated his disposal procedure, and then took the black bags outside for the garbage crew to remove. As he watched the truck leaving with his victim's remains, Berdella was filled with certainty; a certainty he hadn't previously had.

He needed to keep killing until he was caught.

SIX

A Full-Time Torturer

To Robert Berdella, his actions weren't just mindless torture and debauchery. On the contrary, in his mind, he was doing something worthwhile, something almost artistic or scientific; he was studying and experimenting on the human body like few ever had. In reality, his desires were the reason for his actions, and Berdella was able to justify his actions by thinking of them in this way.

Only three months later, the next victim lay chained in Berdella's home. This time our killer wanted to escalate the severity of his methods.

On September 26, 1985, Berdella received a telephone call from a man known as Walter James Ferris, who had already spent time at his home on a previous occasion. Ferris wished to stay at

Berdella's for a short period again, which Berdella found extremely convenient. His next victim had arrived, without him even looking for one. In fact, Berdella would later admit that Ferris was the first man he'd taken home with the intention to torture, unlike his other three victims. In their cases, he had been unaware of what his true intentions were, until they were within the walls of his house.

For this visit, Berdella and Walter met at a bar. They chatted and had a few drinks together before returning to Berdella's house. Once in the privacy of his home, Berdella immediately drugged Ferris with tranquilizers and tied him to his bed, where he would be tortured repeatedly for 27 hours. His previous torture of Mark Wallace via electrical shocks had increased Berdella's appetite for this method of inducing pain. He soon began to subject the struggling Ferris to 7,700-volt shocks—both to his shoulders and testicles, each shock lasting as long as five minutes.

Berdella also continued where he'd left off with the hypodermic needles, ramming several into Ferris's neck and genitals, all the while making notes in his diary. He made sure to document even the smallest details, studying the reactions caused by different abuse to individual parts of the man's body.

Eventually, Berdella pushed Walter too hard; the man could no longer sit up or breathe properly. It seemed that Berdella had used an excessive amount of sedative. Consequently, Walter's breathing failed and he died soon after. Berdella added a note in his diary indicating the end of another so-called 'project.'

Berdella felt contented with his studies, despite Ferris's untimely death. He rapidly dissected his victim's body in the upstairs bathroom, disposing of the corpse piece by piece into separate black bags. Again, the garbage crew ensured he remained undetected and soon Berdella was back to living his normal life.

Months passed and Berdella attempted to concentrate on his life. However, his desires to cause pain and to study the human body through torture inevitably lead him back to his dark activities. Still, it wasn't until the following year, in June 1986, that he managed to capture another victim.

Young Todd Stoops, a 21-year-old male sex worker who Berdella had known since 1984, was next in line to die. Stoops was not the typical victim, however. Amazingly, he had already identified Berdella as the perpetrator of the murders he had read about in the newspaper and whom law enforcement were hunting down. Nevertheless, something (most likely Berdella himself) convinced the young man to go to Berdella's home. Berdella felt great physical attraction towards Todd and this caused him to make his torture of the youth more 'intimate.'

Todd was the first victim to be held for more than just a few days — the young man suffered humiliating indecencies for two whole weeks before his death.

Berdella's methods had evolved even further. He now had total control of his captive through fear and pain. He didn't need to exclusively incapacitate Todd with sedatives, instead combining them with the threat of horrible acts, such as administering electrical shocks through Todd's eyes in an attempt to blind him, and starving him to the point of not even allowing the captive a glass of water. On one particular occasion, after failing to blind the young man, Berdella injected Drano into Todd's larynx, believing he could damage it and leave the youth mute. It was unsuccessful, but the agony was constant and unrelenting.

As if all of these terrible acts weren't enough, Berdella used Todd as a sexual slave, raping and assaulting him constantly during the two weeks he held the man captive. He even forced his fist and forearm up Stoops' rectum, rupturing it. Berdella documented all of this, his Polaroid collection growing larger and his diary filling with more and more notes, all of which meant something to him and his 'studies.'

Todd Stoops grew so weak with fever, blood loss, and sickness that he could barely breathe. Eventually his body gave in; he died in the first week of July 1986, becoming yet another mound of limbs and remains to be thrown into black bags and taken to the garbage out back by Berdella.

Berdella felt happy with himself after Stoops' ordeal and death. He had come so far and accomplished so much more than what he had expected, but the feeling of invincibility remained. After inflicting so much pain and killing several men, he was still a free man; no consequences of any kind weighed him down. In fact, he could keep going if he wanted to and nobody would stand in his way. Furthermore, he had discovered how impressive the human body was and how much damage it could sustain before failing. There was so much more to do; so much more pain to inflict.

Berdella was now convinced: he was nowhere near done. His next victim was going to suffer even more than his last, and he was going to enjoy it even more.

Unfortunately, his desires would become reality not long after. Berdella's urges were worsening, his violence escalating. There were no limits to his capabilities.

SEVEN

No Mercy

The year 1987 arrived. Berdella hadn't tortured or killed anyone since July of the previous year, and it was weighing heavily on him. He led a normal life, but the monster in his mind — that had gradually grown over the years and that needed to be fed intermittently — was whispering dark thoughts to him and begging him to find a new victim.

Berdella had experienced the great pleasure of humiliating, hurting, and killing men, and would now find it very difficult to stop willingly. It was too late; he had gone too far and it was just a matter of how long he could continue before he was detected.

Thus, 20-year-old Larry Wayne Pearson became Berdella's unfortunate next victim.

Larry met Berdella at his store, where he had been immediately attracted to the nature of his wares. He, too, was a collector of esoteric objects, as well as a practitioner of witchcraft. Robert immediately took a liking to the young man, perhaps seeing a younger version of himself standing there in front of him.

A friendship began to develop and Berdella allowed the young man to stay at his home. At first, Berdella did not see Pearson as his next victim, simply allowing the youth to perform different chores around the house in lieu of rent. Berdella was content, Larry was comfortable, and everything was okay.

That is, until Larry made a big mistake.

On June 23, Berdella bailed Larry out of jail. He'd gotten in trouble and Berdella was quick to help him out. As the two returned home, Berdella heard Larry make a distasteful joke about robbing gay men in Wichita. This joke, and Larry's tone when making it, offended Berdella and lowered his opinion of this young man who was staying in his home.

Berdella didn't allow his expression to change, but Larry's words had angered him. The monster within him shifted and awakened. It was too late to stop his desires from rising to the surface; Larry was already a dead man walking.

Berdella waited until that evening to make his move. He plied the young man with drinks until Larry became intoxicated, Berdella wondering all the while how he would begin his latest experiment. Once the young man was drunk, Berdella took action. He injected Pearson with chlorpromazine and dragged him down to the basement, tying the young man's hands above his head and securing the rope to a column. Then he pulled out a syringe. In it he had drain cleaner destined to be applied to Pearson's larynx in a new attempt at rendering one of his victims mute.

Once he was done injecting the chemical product into Larry's voice box, Berdella went upstairs to get his electrical transformer, which he would use to shock Pearson into terror and submission.

Terror and submission were the two key themes of Pearson's time in captivity. He attempted to coax Berdella into treating him well and perhaps even letting him go. He tried to cooperate with the torturer, allowing him to take sexual advantage of him, and withstanding extensive physical abuse without complaint. Berdella used constant and repeated electrical shocks on Larry while documenting their effects on his mind and body, even breaking the young man's right hand to ensure he remained under his control.

On the fifth day, Berdella began to appreciate Pearson's collaboration and allowed him to continue his ordeal in the second-floor bedroom. He did not endure lesser pain and suffering by any means, but his fear of returning to the basement kept him submissive long after he had been taken upstairs.

The torture lasted for six whole weeks, with Berdella taking more detailed notes than ever. He recorded every single thing he did to Larry, as well as the effects of said actions. He added to his collection of Polaroids with graphic pictures of Pearson, most showing his face contorted in agony and mouth hanging open as he gasped in pain.

Larry tried hard to cooperate in the hope of saving his life — even avoiding moving a single muscle while sleeping or being tortured, in an attempt to keep Berdella from increasing the pain — but it wasn't enough. It became too much for Pearson, who increasingly felt frustrated with his captivity and mistreatment. He had been holding back, allowing Berdella to humiliate, rape, and brutalize him in many ways, but it didn't seem to be getting him any closer to freedom. Finally, Berdella pushed young Larry Pearson over the edge. On August 5, 1987, the last time Berdella came to his room and attempted to torture him, Pearson resisted, lashing out and attempting to fight back.

It was useless. He was too well-bound and too weak to accomplish anything. Berdella, in his fury, savagely bludgeoned the young man into unconsciousness, put a bag over his head, and suffocated him to death with a ligature. It angered him to have had to kill Pearson, but he would not accept losing control of his captive, even for an instant. Absolute dominance was an integral part of the house rules he imposed; no man would resist him once captured.

The dead captive was taken downstairs to the dreaded basement, where he was dissected. Berdella, in an act of either rage or triumph, severed the corpse's head from its shoulders and put it aside. Once he was done disposing of the body, Berdella went out back and dug up something he'd kept in his yard for a while: Robert Sheldon's skull. He pushed it aside, replacing it in the hole with Pearson's skull. Then, neatly covering the hole, he returned indoors with Sheldon's skull, cleaning it and removing the teeth. These were kept in envelopes in several locations around the room, while the skull itself was placed inside a closet as a souvenir.

Berdella sat back and reflected on what he'd done. His torturing method had been refined and improved since he'd taken his first captive, Jerry Howell. He'd learned how effective electrical shocks were for keeping a victim submissive and that psychological torture was just as effective as physical and sexual types. There was little that a captive could do when faced with the constant terror of pain and suffering. After all, Berdella never let them know when they were going to die or if they were going to be released at all. Playing with their dwindling hope for survival was key to keeping them reluctant to resist him.

Although Berdella had perfected the art of torture, unfortunately that didn't mean he was going to stop anytime soon. He was long past caring.

As stated previously, from Berdella's perspective, there was a sense of shifted guilt. According to Berdella's logic, it wasn't just him who was guilty of these crimes; it was also law enforcement's fault for not catching him. He had cut out clippings from a local newspaper detailing the case of the missing Jerry Howell, so he was up-to-speed with the investigations. He found it laughable that, despite the fact that he'd been questioned as a prime suspect not long after Howell and Walter James Ferris's disappearances, and had even been placed under surveillance, the local police still hadn't been able to make the necessary connections linking him to the murders.

In fact, when Berdella grew tired of the police questioning and surveillance, he used his lawyer to threaten filing harassment accusations against the police. This made law enforcement take a step back and leave him alone.

Berdella thought he was truly invincible; a ghost who walked unseen in plain daylight and who didn't have to worry about the consequences of his actions. He wanted to torture and kill until he grew tired of it, and with an endless pool of young homosexual men to choose from (due to his connections and friendship with said community), he believed that he wouldn't ever have to worry about finding new victims.

However, Berdella was wrong. He was not invincible, and he would not go on killing forever. His next victim would be his last.

In fact, his next victim would be the very reason Berdella met his downfall.

EIGHT

Outsmarted

The last man to enter Berdella's torture dungeon of a home was no fool. Twenty-two-year-old Chris Bryson's experience as a male sex worker had armed him with a quick wit and the ability to get out of sticky situations with ease. It was, perhaps, why he managed to avoid becoming another cut-up corpse departing Berdella's address in black bags, and why he actually managed to fool The Butcher of Kansas City into trusting him and giving him the means to escape.

It all started on the evening of March 29, 1988, at a Greyhound bus station in downtown Kansas City. Berdella was out looking for company, although he had other intentions for his victim-to-be than just a bit of sex. Chris Bryson spotted the lonely man cruising in his vehicle and approached, believing he was hustling the stranger. It was actually the other way round; Berdella had already honed in on the young sex worker and knew full well that he would be taking him home to torture

Chris was pleasantly surprised when Berdella suggested they go to his home, having grown accustomed to servicing his clients in cheap motel rooms and car back seats. He also didn't expect what was to follow.

When they arrived, Berdella sat Chris down in the living room and talked with the youth, trying to get to know him a bit better. The intention of sex was still there, of course, but Berdella was making it interesting.

Eventually, Berdella suggested they go upstairs to the bedroom. He casually mentioned the fact that his three vicious Chow-Chows lived on the lower level of the house, adding that the upstairs floor had a television and more comfortable furniture. Unknowingly, Chris consented and began climbing the steps. As he did, he felt somebody move swiftly to his side.

Berdella was quick and ruthless, smacking Chris in the back of the head with an iron bar before sedating him and dragging him up to his bedroom, where he immediately bound him to the bed. When Chris woke up, he found himself naked and helpless. A smiling Berdella stood over him with his Polaroid. As Chris attempted to find out what was going on, the torture began.

Berdella, as the reader may have noticed, was increasing the brutality of his methods with each new victim, and Chris Bryson was no exception to this rule. He began by fitting a dog collar onto Chris's neck and beat the youth with an iron club, aiming to break bones in his hands and legs. He injected Chris with animal tranquilizer and ensured his continued health with antibiotics to protect the many wounds he'd inflicted on the young man's flesh. Again, Berdella documented what he'd done to Bryson, taking more pictures than ever, and watching the young sex worker's agony with glee.

The first night of torture ended with a long session of brutal rape, including the insertion of objects into the victim's anal cavity.

The next morning was not merciful to Chris. Berdella entered the room and woke him up by jabbing swabs soaked with alcohol into his eyes. He later added ammonia with the intention of making Chris blind. He continued raping the young man, causing him to scream and call out for help. Berdella, always dominant and controlling, quickly grabbed a syringe and injected Drano into Chris' throat, threatening to make him lose his voice entirely. He told Chris that he had tortured and killed several men already. He also told him that the three dogs he'd mentioned on the night

143

before had eaten the captives after Berdella was done with them. Chris believed the tale — a story not so far from the truth, to be fair.

Electricity continued to be a crucial tool in Berdella's torture repertoire; he constantly shocked the young sex worker with alligator clips clamped onto different parts of his body, including his testicles. In the photographs, Bryson's agony is quite clear: his eyes are wide and his body is full of cuts and open wounds. Berdella warned Chris against escaping, telling him that he needed only to think about himself, Berdella, and the house.

After a few days of captivity, Chris seemed to have gained territory with Berdella, who sat on top of him and began to pull out the Polaroids he had taken of his previous victims. Berdella explained to Chris that he had held others in the same situation, and that — if he gained some of Berdella's trust — there was a chance he could save his life and leave captivity. If not, Berdella continued, he would be murdered and disposed of like his predecessors. "I've gotten this far with other people before and they're dead now," the killer said in a cautionary tone, "because of mistakes they made."

By the evening of the third day, Chris noticed that Berdella was certainly starting to trust him. He'd agreed to loosen the bindings on his arms and had tied them in front of him instead of above his head. Next, Chris asked the killer to leave the television on. Berdella allowed Chris to keep the remote control when he was out of the room, and even threw him a cigarette and some matches.

Unlike some of the previous victims, who had pinned their hopes on Berdella being merciful and letting them go, Chris had long abandoned any such expectations. He knew he had to escape, no matter what. It became an obsession, one that would keep him going even when the pain was at its fullest. He watched Berdella closely and kept his eyes and ears open when the man wasn't nearby. The fact that Berdella had given him the remote control meant he could keep the television's volume down and listen to his captor's movements. At one point, he stopped hearing Berdella at all. Robert Berdella — torturer, killer, and captor — had left the house to do some errands.

Fortunately for Chris, the looser arrangement of the ropes that bound him allowed him some leeway to get one of his hands free, a fact that he had confirmed earlier, while Berdella wasn't watching. He listened one last time to make sure that his captor was gone, and then Chris knew:

It was time.

He pulled his hand loose and stretched across the bed, pushing aside the cigarette and grabbing the matches his captor had thrown there. Quickly and anxiously, he lit each one, using them to burn the ropes wrapped around his other limbs so that he could escape.

Each second was vital, for if Berdella returned, Chris knew that he would be killed.

Finally, with the ropes still dangling from his body, the young man stood up to look through the window. He worried about it being locked or nailed closed, but Berdella had not expected any of his captives to escape and hadn't taken such precautions. A two-floor fall separated him from the ground, but Bryson had no time to think about it; his life was in danger. He smashed the window with ease and leapt out, breaking a bone in his foot as he landed. The pain made him grit his teeth, but he knew that even worse pain awaited him if he stayed, so he kept going, running to a house across the street.

There was a man standing in the street, reading a meter. He spotted Bryson and heard the young man screaming at him to call the police. The meter reader decided to leave the problem in someone else's hands and alerted the nearest neighbors instead. They were quick to call the police, although they didn't allow Chris to enter their home due to his state of damage and undress. Luckily for the young victim, the police force was quick to arrive at his location.

Four officers questioned Chris almost immediately. He was forced to lie about his occupation, instead saying that he had been hitchhiking when Berdella had abducted, raped, and tortured him for four days. He described how he'd been injected with drain cleaner, sodomized, and drugged during the entirety of his captivity. His scars, swollen eyes, and the dog collar gave his words the necessary emphasis to give credence to his story. He then told the police officers how he'd escaped out his captor's window.

The officers were quick to swing into action, with some taking Chris to a nearby hospital while the others stayed at the crime scene. They radioed the Kansas City Police Department to request a formal search warrant.

The killer hadn't been arrested yet, but it was already over for him. Chris had succeeded in doing what the six men before him had sadly been unable to do, despite their best resistance.

He had successfully brought Robert Berdella's terror spree to a climactic ending.

Want more? Guess what? You can read the rest for free on Amazon Kindle Unlimited by visiting:

https://amzn.to/2nn6L10

No sign up required. It is 100% free!

Dark Fantasies Turn Reality

For updates about new releases, as well as exclusive promotions, sign up for my newsletter and you can also receive a free book today. Thank you and see you soon.

Sign up here: http://free---book.ryanbeckerwrites.com

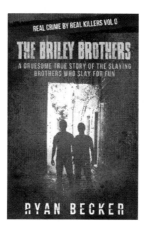

The Briley Brothers: A Gruesome True Story of the Slaying Brothers Who Slay For Fun is a book that recounts the tale of the three murderous brothers (Linwood, James, and Anthony) and their friend and accomplice (Duncan Meekins); the killers were not remembered by their dozen murders but by the brutality with which they took the lives of their victims. There is no other term to describe them but *ruthless,* as you will soon find out.

Prepare yourself, we're not going to hold back on details or cut out any of the gruesome truths...

About the Author

Ryan Becker is a True Crime author who started his writing journey in late 2016. Like most of you, he loves to explore the process of how individuals turn their darkest fantasies into a reality. He has always had a passion for storytelling. So, together with his fascination with psychology and true crime, he aims to tell stories that will make you solve a puzzle in your mind. It is his goal for his readers to experience the full immersion with the dark reality of the world just like how he used to do it in his younger days. Now with his small team, Ryan wishes to push the storytelling even further with other passionate writers and together they can leave a mark on the reader with their various storytelling styles.

Follow Ryan:

Author Website: www.ryanbeckerwrites.com

Twitter: @ryanbeckerwrites

Facebook: www.facebook.com/RyanBeckerWrites/

Amazon: www.amazon.com/author/ryanbecker

46118714R00085

Made in the USA
Columbia, SC
22 December 2018